WOMEN LIVING FEARLESSLY

A COLLECTION BY
PEACE MITCHELL AND KATY GARNER

Women Changing the World Press acknowledges the Elders and Traditional owners of country throughout Australia and their connection to lands, waters and communities. We pay our respect to Elders past and present and extend that respect to all Aboriginal and Islander peoples today. We honour more than sixty thousand years of Indigenous women's voices, stories, leadership and wisdom.

Copyright © Peace Mitchell and Katy Garner
First published in Australia in 2024
by Women Changing the World Press
an imprint of KMD Books
Waikiki, WA 6169

All rights reserved. No part of this book may be used or reproduced by any means, graphic, electronic or mechanical, including photocopying, recording, taping or by any information storage retrieval system without the written permission of the copyright owner except in the case of brief quotations embodied in critical articles and reviews.

Because of the dynamic nature of the Internet, any web addresses or links contained in this book may have changed since publication and may no longer be valid. The views expressed in this work are solely those of the author and do not necessarily reflect the views of the publisher and the publisher hereby disclaims any responsibility for them.

Edited by Tracy Regan

Typeset in Adobe Garamond Pro 12/17pt

 A catalogue record for this work is available from the National Library of Australia

National Library of Australia Catalogue-in-Publication data:
Women Living Fearlessly /Peace Mitchell and Katy Garner

ISBN:
978-1-7636406-7-2
(Paperback)

To those who know they have a greater purpose and are awaiting the permission to live a big life. It's your time and you're ready. Stop waiting. Live fearlessly, chase your dreams and live the life you have imagined. The world needs your magic.

CONTENTS

INTRODUCTION 1

ANDREA CARTER
IGNITING INNER CONFIDENCE THROUGH TRUST AND BELIEF 13

ANNA ABESADZE
ECHOES OF SELF-DOUBT CONQUERING IMPOSTER SYNDROME 27

BERNADETTE ALONZO CORTES
FROM BROWN MONKEY TO LEGALLY BROWN FROM SPOILED LITTLE BRAT TO A FIGHTER OF THE OPPRESSED 41

BETHANY CHAMBERS
SURVIVOR NOT VICTIM 57

DR DALE LAING-HALL
SIGNIFICANTLY SEEN EMPOWERING SELF AND OTHERS 75

ELLIE D. SHEFI
BE BOLD, LIVE FEARLESSLY 87

FARAH MAK
DEAR YOUNGER ME 103

FLORENCE KAYUNGWA
THE BOLD AND BEAUTIFUL 115

IRIS MHLANGA
SHATTERING GLASS CEILINGS 129

JUSTINE COX
A JOURNEY OF STRENGTH AND KINDNESS MY PATH TO RELATIONSHIP-CENTRED LEADERSHIP AND BACK TO ME 141

KATY GARNER
LIVING FEARLESSLY IS NOT THE ABSENCE OF FEAR, BUT THE COURAGE TO FACE IT 155

KELLY SMEATH
DREAM BIG; ANYTHING IS POSSIBLE! 165

LIZ COURTNEY
CHANGING SHOES, CHANGING WORLDS ONE MOTHER'S JOURNEY FROM WORKING IN STILETTOES TO TRAVELLING THE WORLD AND DIRECTING 175

LISA GAL
FEARLESSLY EMBRACING LIFE'S OPPORTUNITIES 189

MAFAE YUNON - BELASCO
FEAR - FALSE EVIDENCE APPEARING REAL 199

MERCEDES SORIA
COURAGE ACROSS CONTINENTS TALES OF RESILIENCE 207

PATRICIA GONDE
FROM SHADOWS TO SPOTLIGHT 221

PINAR SEKMEN
THE POWER OF UNLEARNING 237

RUVIMBO MAZONDE
THE JOURNEY TO BECOME 249

SANDRA SPADANUDA
FROM DARKNESS TO EMPOWERMENT MY FIGHT FOR JUSTICE 263

SAMANTHA J.
FROM BROKENNESS TO UNSTOPPABLE STRENGTH RECLAIMING MY WORTH
AND BUILDING A PREMIUM BRAND 277

SARA KNIGHT
SURVIVAL MODE TO THRIVING MODE 291

SARAH MACRAE
RISING FROM THE ASHES A PHOENIX IN THE MAKING 305

SOFIA CALVO NIÑO
EVEN 319

TARA CROKER
MY STORY 'BUNYANDYI GILANG' 335

TIFFANY JAMES
ROARING INTO AUTHENTICITY 347

VERONICA (VEE) HASLAM
THE GIFT OF SILENCE 361

INTRODUCTION

F ear oh constant companion,
   Always there to remind us to stay small, stay silent, stay safe.
If we all listened to everything our fear told us nothing would ever get done! It wants us to hide away our gifts and our magic, our radiance and our brilliance, our true essence, our spirit, our purpose and passions.

Fear wants us to lock up all of that talent and potential in a box and keep it hidden away from anyone and everyone in a misguided attempt at keeping us from harm, from shame, from humiliation and from criticism of any kind.

Holding us back from sharing our voice, holding us back from sharing our ideas, holding us back from making new friends, exploring new lands, trying new career paths even following our dreams.

Holding us back and holding us back and holding us back, again and again, over and over.

But what if we stopped letting that happen, What if we shouted 'STOP' and demanded that our fear stay small and silent and hidden in a box instead? What if we believed in ourselves and our radiance and our brilliance and our magic? What if we stood up to fear, stepped over fear, silenced fear and then went ahead and followed our dreams anyway?

What does it mean to be fearless?

To live a life without fear? How would that even be possible?

In truth, I don't think it's completely possible, however I know that we can learn to not be held back by our fear. The fear still exists of course

INTRODUCTION

but it doesn't have to have the same power over us.

When I think of fearlessness I think of other brave women I've been blessed to know in my life. Women who haven't altogether conquered their fear but those who have been afraid and done things anyway. One of my favourite reflections on her relationship with fear is this one:

"Dearest Fear,

Creativity and I are about to go on a road trip together. I understand you'll be joining us, because you always do. I do acknowledge that you believe you have an important job to do in my life, and that your take your job seriously.

Apparently your job is to induce complete panic whenever I'm about to do anything interesting – and, may I say, you are superb at your job. So by all means, keep doing your job, if you feel you must. But I will also be doing my job on this road trip, which is to work hard and stay focused. And Creativity will be doing its job, which is to remain stimulating and inspiring.

There's plenty of room in this vehicle for all of us, so make yourself at home, but understand this: Creativity and I are the only ones who will be making any decisions along the way. I recognize and respect that you are part of this family, and I will never exclude you from our activities, but still – your suggestions will never be followed. You're allowed to have a seat, and you're allowed to have a voice, but you are not allowed to have a vote. You're not allowed to touch the road maps; you're not allowed to suggest detours; you're not allowed to fiddle with the temperature. Dude, you're not even allowed to touch the radio.

But above all else, my dear old familiar friend, you are absolutely forbidden to drive."

Elizabeth Gilbert, Big Magic

I love how playfully Liz addresses her fear, after reading many of her books and hearing her speak, I know that fear has been a part of her life since she was a little girl, always there, always trying to keep her small

WOMEN LIVING FEARLESSLY

and silent and safe. And yet she has achieved so much by defying that voice, standing up to that voice, silencing that voice and not letting fear control her.

It's not always easy to silence the voice of fear, when I reflect on my greatest moments of fear I realise that inside me burned a greater fire; a fire to keep going, to believe in myself, to get up after every fall and to listen to the quiet voice of reassurance and knowing inside that whispers 'you've got this, you can do it, you have everything you need.'

Imagine if all women knew that they had the power to silence their fears. It would be amazing. It would literally change the world and women everywhere would be blown away by their potential and what they could achieve if they gave themselves the permission to live the life of their dreams.

When we are brave enough to live fearlessly, we experience the rewards of a courageous life. We finally discover that we have the power to follow our dreams, to realise our potential, to live our best and most beautiful lives.

IGNITING INNER CONFIDENCE THROUGH TRUST AND BELIEF

Andrea Carter

The quest for fearless living becomes a beacon of hope and empowerment in a world often overshadowed by fear, doubt and uncertainty. This chapter is for those who feel metaphorically and physically different from others, so that you discover how to empower every fibre of belief about your worth and value. This is a chapter dedicated to understanding and harnessing the power of trust, grit and belief to illuminate our lives from within.

UNDERSTAND THEN DEFY LEARNED HELPLESSNESS

I was born into a family of immigrants. As a first-generation Canadian, the goal was never to stand out but instead to conform, keep my head down, work hard and make something of myself, all while doing everything possible to be 'like the neighbours' and fit in as much as possible. But by the age of twelve, I had already lost at the proverbial game of 'keeping up with the Jones'. I stood out. At five feet, eleven inches tall, I towered above my friends and family, including my parents. While height may have been the visible element that separated me from my siblings, parents and extended family, the way I thought, what I valued and how I behaved highlighted the distance between us even more. From the tender age of twelve, I had dreams and ideas of how to make the world a better place because I felt that was the point of human existence – to leave this world better for having lived. The beauty of difference and standing out is that your viewpoint is also considerably different. I desperately want to change what happens to people when that automatic silence creeps in, the silence that accompanies the downward gaze of eyes associated with someone different trying to interact and contribute to a conversation with an 'ingroup' or group of monolithic people. The changing of the subject or talking over you when you vocalise differences of opinion. The persistent denial, misdirection, contradiction and even lying by those who are 'normal' or 'fit in' make the person who is different doubt their thoughts, memories and experiences. While I would encounter many of these experiences throughout my lifetime, sports in my teenage years introduced an internal power to trust and keep trying that consistently pulled me out of the alternative 'learned helplessness'. My desire for this change grew stronger and louder when both my children surpassed my height on their twelfth birthdays and began experiencing similar social exclusions. I knew I had to find ways to dismantle 'learned helplessness'.

The term 'learned helplessness', first coined in the 1960s by Martin Seligman and Steven Maier, was incited from experiments with dogs that demonstrate that animals exposed to inescapable electric shocks eventually stop trying to escape, even when later placed in situations where escape was possible. The behaviour suggests that the dogs had 'learned' to be helpless. People who repeatedly experience exclusion and ostracisation or have their differences consistently highlighted and their value deflated are prone to learned helplessness. For example, take women in the workplace who are repeatedly challenged for their skills, knowledge or expertise. Women who consistently face obstacles in career advancement, being overlooked for promotions, not receiving recognition for contributions or encountering consistent bias and discrimination. And when they finally receive recognition, it is often laced with conditions and minimisations. Over time, these women come to believe that their efforts are pointless, leading most to stop seeking new opportunities or advocating for themselves. Even when opportunities for growth or change arise, they may not pursue them, having internalised the experiences to believe their actions won't make a difference.

While this example remains rampant today, it's not just women in corporations who experience this. Every person, depending on their identities and the identities of the ingroup, will come up against bias and discrimination in environments where differences exist. It's a social cycle that can limit our potential, causing it to go unrealised and further deepen our sense of helplessness.

While societal conditioning begs people to fit in, conform and assimilate, dismantling their confidence and value, I encourage you to learn how to break this cycle that enables potential learned helplessness for yourself, and then create spaces where you can model this for others.

HOW DO WE DEFY LEARNED HELPLESSNESS?

Look at each challenging downward glaze, interruption or act of exclusion as a challenge to sharpen your creativity, innovation and problem-solving skills, helping you define your bigger goals and vision for your life.

As cliché as this statement is, its value lies in its accuracy, 'Just like diamonds are formed under immense pressure, your true brilliance shines the brightest in the face of adversity.' Instead of personalising someone's bias, judgement or acts of exclusion as something 'less than' within yourself, notice what you are challenging the homogenous ingroup to look at. Trust that your brilliance is meant to leave a footprint on this world for the greater good, and in the face of adversity, never lose sight of your value and worth. Let setbacks or challenges serve as a reminder of your unwavering spirit. Wherever you are starting from today, define a goal and vision for your life. Get out a piece of paper and write down your goal and vision for the year, so you have something concrete to work towards. Then, when adversity strikes, challenge the act against you by getting creative about how you handle the situation. Instead of letting the act diminish your confidence, worth or value, convert the energy into fuel to think outside the box and find innovative solutions. Adapt the mindset that every challenge is an opportunity to grow stronger, wiser and more connected to your goal and vision. By staying true to yourself, you define your own path and purpose, and can remain resilient in adversity. By taking these steps, you'll defy learned helplessness and carve out a path that reflects your brilliance. With all its ups and downs, your journey will ultimately define your legacy, and you are constantly deciding what that will add to.

DARKNESS IS NOT DISPELLED BY CHASING IT AWAY BUT BY BRINGING IN THE LIGHT

Recently, I was in a situation where I was a parent chaperone for a high-level teenage girl sporting event that provided five days of elite training and then three days of top competition. In these situations, teams are generated ahead of time, elite athletes are selected from all over the province, and then they have five days to learn how to work together, develop their skills and grow as a team. While most teams acquired the values and behaviours of being a good teammate and creating an inclusive environment that supports each person's talent, the team my daughter was assigned to had coaches who were more focused on skill-building than team environment. What quickly took place was that ingroup and outgroup behaviour enabled the girls to choose between honouring their worth or being liked and part of the ingroup. Anyone who did not conform received the silent treatment, small acts of exclusion and glaring looks of blame and shame when they were not perfect in their execution. While all girls made mistakes, the ones who did not conform were the ones who were tortured with silence and exclusion. In this example, you can see how leadership impacts the behaviours of a team. It took one day for the first girl to drop out, saying she was homesick – one more day for multiple injuries to occur.

By the time they got to the first day of competition, the ingroup had the power of one look to induce extreme learned helplessness. The first match, I watched in horror as my daughter, trying to control her anxiety around these players, scratched her skin on the court to the point of bleeding, while the coaches turned their heads to ignore it. Parents and spectators gasped, but no-one did anything. I sat in horror and disbelief that this behaviour had happened right before me. Once the match ended, I immediately pulled her off the court and into the hallway. At that moment, we had a choice; allow the darkness and negativity of ingroup behaviour to chase away the light and brilliance within us or shine brighter to overcome it. While difference and darkness, in many forms, often engulf people's lives because they cast a shadow of fear, doubt and despair, I have learned that darkness and exclusion are not dispelled by chasing them away but instead by bringing in the light.

HOW DO WE MAKE OUR LIGHT MORE SIGNIFICANT THAN THE DARKNESS?

Your brain is an incredible organ that is often underleveraged. In a situation like this, where the negativity of others feels more prominent than your capacity, start by recalling a past success and remember how your worth was more significant than the challenge. When you do this, your brain engages in a complex interplay of memory retrieval, emotional processing, cognitive reappraisal, motivation and stress regulation.

When I pulled my daughter aside, I reminded her of when she started with a new team and her skill level was lower than the team. In that setting, while her peers cared about her and her wellbeing, she needed to create a goal and vision that allowed her to succeed. That year, her goal was to meet their skill level by the end of the year, choosing in the face of each challenge to learn instead of judging herself. I reminded her that by the end of her season, she had won the coach award in the club, the principal's award at school and was a two-time champion in her sport. I gave her the option; you could allow this experience to engulf you because you can't change them, or you could let your light and determination be more significant and lead by example. There's no revenge or begging for acceptance, it's merely you growing your light and determination so big, that they can't help but acknowledge the potential of working differently.

From a brain perspective, reminding my daughter of her successes allowed her to approach the challenge confidently, clearly and with grit, increasing her resilience and likelihood of success. I encouraged her to remember how fun it was to play her sport, how it felt to learn and grow, and that no matter what, her presence alone brought tremendous value to the team. Through those mechanisms, her brain helped her overcome her immediate obstacle and reinforced a mindset that helped her prepare for future challenges she would face in the next matches. She carried her team into playoffs and ultimately won bronze in the games.

Your inner light, often called your confidence, grit, resilience or the unique essence that defines who you are, is like a seed that needs careful nurturing to grow. While it is the core of what makes you distinctly you, it still requires attention and care to flourish. To increase your inner light, you must do the work of self-reflection, embracing challenges, learning from failures and consistently pushing beyond your comfort zone. When we got home from the elite games, we sat down and deeply studied what we learned. My daughter reflected on how she would quickly get down on herself, as she constantly looked for approval from her teammates instead of believing in herself. Can you relate to this? While the example might seem juvenile, the concept applies to everyone. Consider how often you give external opinions more weight and value than your internal beliefs. Too often, those with the power to act, ignore injustice. In these moments, we can't rely on others to save us. It's crucial to strengthen the ability to prioritise our internal beliefs and drown out biased external opinions.

LEARNING TO LISTEN TO YOURSELF OVER THE OPINIONS OF OTHERS

A cardinal rule of growing your inner light is knowing who to listen to and when someone else's insights will help you grow versus tear you down. To increase your light more significantly than the darkness, always recognise that people will give you their opinion without it being solicited, and sometimes, as a means to put you down. Once we understand that this is simply a process of societal conditioning and dated programming, the opportunity to reroute your neural impulses and pay more attention to your inner voice and light is possible. An opinion stems from personal bias, emotion and limited perspective without evidence, critical thinking or deep understanding. While everyone is entitled to their opinion, they can be shallow and unsubstantiated if not backed by knowledge, experience or careful consideration. Always keep this in mind when you are learning, doing something new or different, trying on a new role, market or workplace, or facing challenges.

True wisdom and knowledge require constant open-mindedness, a willingness to engage with different viewpoints, the ability to question assumptions and the desire to seek out facts when faced with insurmountable challenges. Never rely solely on the opinions of others who are not in your shoes; their superficial thinking is based on limited understanding. Instead, choose to look for growth, empathy and meaningful dialogue that helps you grow your confidence and maximise your inner light.

I used to think that confidence was something you either had or didn't, like a talent you were born with. But with education, research and practical application, I have learned that confidence is something you build, like a muscle, through experiences, reflections and sometimes environments that do not have your best intention at heart. Igniting inner confidence isn't about pretending to be fearless, it's about seeing the challenges, embracing your fears and choosing to move forward despite them. In these moments, when the world tries to diminish your light, you can consciously decide to shine even brighter. Trusting yourself comes from nurturing these processes and showing yourself that your abilities aren't just abstract concepts but your lifelines. When the world feels too overwhelming, too critical or dismissive of your worth, you still have tools and options to leverage to move forward.

To truly live fearlessly, you must first learn to trust yourself. Trust does not happen from one experience; internal trust is built slowly, over time, as you push through challenges and celebrate even the most minor victories. Each time you confront a fear or overcome a setback, you lay another brick in the foundation of your self-confidence. It's not about *never failing* because that will happen too, it's about understanding that failure is a part of the journey and that each failure brings you one step closer to your goals. When you start to believe in yourself, you stop needing external validation. You stop looking for approval from those who would never understand your journey, and you start focusing on your growth and path.

In a world that often tells us to conform, play it safe and fit in, choosing to trust and believe in yourself is a bold act of self-empowerment that ignites your inner confidence. It's a declaration that you are enough, just as you are, and that your unique light has a purpose. By nurturing this inner belief and consistently choosing to trust yourself, you can ignite confidence so strong that it guides you and inspires others to find their light. Let's make this your time for learned confidence to outweigh any molecule of learned helplessness. Together … let's live fearlessly!

Andrea Carter is a recognised expert in workplace culture, specialising in bridging the gap between culture and equity, diversity and inclusion (EDI) through the concept of belonging. Recently appointed to the Forbes Council, Andrea is celebrated for her ability to create transformative organisational cultures that drive engagement, innovation and performance. As a strategic advisor, she partners with leadership teams to address cultural challenges, implementing neuroscience-based strategies, statistical analysis and tactical solutions to foster environments where every employee feels valued, respected, and included.

In her role as an adjunct professor at Adler University, Andrea teaches leadership, industrial and organisational psychology and advanced statistical analysis. Her academic achievements include a master's degree in industrial and organisational psychology with a concentration in human resources management and a specialisation in corporate social justice. She is also certified in MAXQDA and SPSS.

With over eighteen years of experience in neuroscience-based learning and development, Andrea designs and delivers innovative EDIB training programs grounded in research. Her work includes co-authoring the largest study in the Canadian mining industry, involving over 3,500 participants from thirteen TSX-listed companies, where she identified key indicators for enhancing EDIB strategies and developing diverse talent pipelines.

Andrea's contributions to the field have earned her multiple accolades, including first place in the Micro Business of the Year category for her consulting firm, Belonging First, which sets benchmarks for

ANDREA CARTER

organisational practices centred on belonging. Additionally, she was awarded second place in the Innovation Award category for her groundbreaking research and innovative approach to fostering belonging in the workplace.

In the 2024/2025 academic year, Andrea will lead the inaugural Belonging in the Workplace program for the Institute of Visionary Leadership and Organizational Health, in partnership with Fulbright Canada, a prestigious opportunity extended to groundbreaking researchers. Her work integrates cutting-edge research and offers executives, HR leaders and managers practical tools to enhance organisational culture, improve performance outcomes and create thriving, inclusive workplaces.

For more information about Andrea's research at Adler University, visit: adler.edu/2024/05/31/women-changing-the-world-honours-adler-university-adjunct-faculty-andrea-carter-with-two-prestigious-awards/

To read her latest article in *The Conversation*, visit: adler.edu/2024/09/03/in-the-face-of-dei-backlash-belonging-plays-a-key-role-to-future-success/

For more on Andrea's work and consulting firm, visit: belongingfirst.com

Her Forbes profile is available at: councils.forbes.com/profile/Andrea-Carter-CEO-Founder-Belonging-First/efe4f605-e87d-4d88-bd24-3acce4c01ba9

ECHOES OF SELF-DOUBT
CONQUERING IMPOSTER SYNDROME

Anna Abesadze

Have you ever found yourself wondering if you are truly good enough or if your success was just a stroke of luck? What will happen if people discover the 'real me'?

If you find yourself consistently downplaying your accomplishments, doubting your abilities to the point of feeling like a fraud, know that you're not alone. Would it be comforting to know that even highly accomplished people, like Albert Einstein, Michelle Obama, Maya Angelou, Emma Watson and Natalie Portman, have struggled with imposter syndrome despite their remarkable success and recognition?

In the realm of imposter syndrome, there lies a harsh reality; its pervasive negative thoughts can affect every corner of our lives. While self-criticality and humility can be admirable traits, crossing the line into excessive self-doubt could lead to diminished self-confidence and missed opportunities for growth and success.

How can we leverage imposter syndrome to enhance our strength instead of diminishing it?

Should we view imposter syndrome as a friend or an enemy? The choice is entirely ours. I've learned that if you search for reasons why you're not good enough, you'll always find them. Conversely, if you consistently seek out the best in yourself, you'll discover it readily. It all boils down to our attitude. As Henry Ford famously said, 'Whether you think you can, or you think you can't – you're right.'

NAVIGATING SELF-DOUBT THROUGH JOURNALLING

At 3:30pm, the phone rang, breaking the afternoon silence. On the other end, a voice delivered the news I'd been dreaming of for as long as I could remember: I had won the exchange program to the USA and would be spending my senior year of high school there, all expenses paid. My heart raced as I imagined the endless possibilities and new experiences awaiting me. I felt like I was floating on air, my dream finally becoming a reality.

As the initial wave of euphoria subsided, doubts began to creep in. Did they really call me, or had I imagined it? Was this just an illusion? If it was real, why had they chosen me? The other candidates were exceptional – did I truly deserve this opportunity? My mind swirled with questions; a mixture of self-doubt and astonished disbelief, as I grappled with the enormity of what had just happened.

Even after achieving significant career milestones, those struggling with imposter syndrome continue to wrestle with feelings of insecurity and self-doubt.

Back then, without the internet to Google strategies for coping with imposter syndrome, I didn't even realise what it was or that others faced the same challenges. In the solitude of my struggle, I stumbled upon a strategy that would become my saving grace.

In my quest for validation, I found myself desperately searching for reasons why I deserved the victory. So, I started a journal – a chronicle of my journey. I meticulously documented every small achievement, clipping out every mention in school and local newspapers where my name appeared. With each entry, I felt a renewed sense of purpose. The journal became a map of my triumphs, guiding me through the labyrinth of doubt. It reminded me of the countless small victories that paved the way to my greatest successes.

The struggles of self-doubt haunted me at every turn of success – the scholarship for my BA studies, the prestigious presidential scholarship for academic excellence during my undergraduate years and even when I secured a full-ride scholarship for my MA at Tallinn University. Surprisingly, amidst these achievements, I found myself questioning: *How did the committee choose me? What if they discover I'm not as capable as they think?* Yet, two years later, I not only graduated with honours and received academic accolades, but also had the honour of being invited to a reception hosted by the Estonian president as a top student. This was alongside successful internships and leadership roles within university societies.

Recounting this matters because reflecting on these fears reveals a pattern; similar doubts plagued me at the beginning of each endeavour, only to be surpassed by success. These experiences gradually built my confidence and self-trust.

Keeping a journal transcends mere documentation – it's a transformative practice that validates your achievements and provides clarity on your goals. By documenting successes, large and small, you build a concrete record of progress and capability, crucial for combating imposter syndrome and affirming your worth. Reflecting on these achievements cultivates positivity, celebrating strengths and reducing anxieties. Even without self-doubt, journalling fosters goal-setting, accountability and confidence, guiding personal growth with clarity and purpose.

EMBRACING IMPERFECTION: LESSONS IN COURAGE, GROWTH AND RESILIENCE

In all our endeavours, it's essential to remember that perfection is an unattainable goal. Embracing this truth frees us from the constraints of perfectionism, allowing us to take risks and explore new opportunities. It's through these experiences that we grow and move forward. As Mark Zuckerberg said, 'The greatest successes come from having the freedom to fail.' So, grant yourself that freedom and view each failure as a lesson bringing you closer to your goal. Wisdom, fortunately or unfortunately, doesn't come from age, but from the experiences we live through.

On the journey to becoming who we want to be, we often encounter versions of ourselves that we might not always like. Is this part of the process? Absolutely. It's inevitable that we'll walk thorny paths, face heartbreak and not enjoy every chapter of our lives.

In the story of my life, I've often found myself on the edge of new beginnings, waiting for a perfect moment that never came. In that hesitation, I missed out on so many chances to grow and move forward, each opportunity slipping away, leaving only the ache of what could have been.

Those grappling with impostor syndrome often place an undue burden on themselves, expecting flawless performance and fearing that any mistake will expose them as undeserving of their success. Embracing imperfection means acknowledging that flaws are inherent and do not diminish our worth or achievements.

Do we ever broadcast our defeats and setbacks? Is it not only the victories that make the headlines? Have you ever seen a social media post about not getting a job or failing an exam? It's easy to overlook that even the most successful individuals have a past marked by numerous failures. Yet, what sets them apart is their resilience – they never surrendered. Isn't there a certain beauty in that journey, even in the moments where effort doesn't quite translate into success?

Throughout my career, I've been fortunate to explore and work as an educational professional in five different countries, granting me a rich, multicultural experience. If I had let perfectionism hold me back, I would never have achieved my dream job or found the courage to return to my homeland with a mission to give back and drive change. Stepping out of my comfort zone required immense courage. I realise how much I would have missed if I had doubted my abilities.

Working closely with senior leadership teams has taught me a valuable truth; no-one starts with all the answers. The journey unfolds with perseverance, genuine intentions and hard work, revealing perspectives and solutions along the way. When entering a long tunnel, do you see the light right away? Big goals are like that – the bigger they are, the more focused you must be, working harder and walking further to discover the light.

Remember, this journey isn't about becoming perfect; it's about seeing the beauty in your efforts and acknowledging that you are enough, just as you are.

CHALLENGE NEGATIVE THOUGHTS

From my life experience, I have met many individuals with every skill and expertise needed to succeed, yet they remained far from where they aspired to be. They were prisoners of their own minds, held back by negative thinking that hindered their progress.

Events and experiences hold the meanings we attach to them. If we approach a meeting with the preconceived notion that it will be unimportant, that will likely be our reality. However, if we seek out even small benefits and aim to glean something valuable, we will. When I was a freshman and junior at university, I took on free internships and volunteer opportunities. I never doubted their worth and ended up gaining invaluable experiences that continue to benefit me. In contrast, some peers dismissed these opportunities as a waste of time and, consequently, missed out on those benefits. Were we both right? Perhaps. Our beliefs shaped our experiences and outcomes.

My life journey proves that thoughts matter immensely. When you're emotionally invested in your goals, your energy and determination propel you toward success. My philosophy is to give my best in every endeavour and maintain a positive outlook. Commitment is crucial, not just for achieving results but for the tranquility it brings to your soul.

During my career in the USA, I embraced a piece of wisdom, that while we may not control the events that befall us, we hold the power to shape our responses. Life is a tapestry woven with both joyous and challenging surprises, and the essence of living is to do our part diligently and hope for the best.

Positive affirmations are a powerful tool; they are not magic, but a guiding light. We must work hard for our dreams, knowing that affirmations alone won't conjure miracles. Behind every success lies a backdrop of mundane routine, executed with admirable discipline. Embrace this and believe you are born under a shining star. In time, it will become your reality.

By consistently challenging negative thoughts, you gradually loosen the hold of imposter syndrome on your life. Imagine the self-doubt that once felt like a heavy chain starting to break apart. Each time you question a negative belief about yourself, you chip away at that chain. This process builds your confidence, helping you recognise and embrace your true capabilities. As you foster a healthier and more realistic self-perception, you begin to see yourself through a lens of compassion and truth.

SWIMMING AGAINST THE CURRENT: FINDING STRENGTH THROUGH IMPOSTER SYNDROME

There are good things that imposter syndrome has taught me too. Due to the doubts, I was always proving my worth, battling the whispers of inadequacy with relentless effort. I worked tirelessly, my heart set on making my dreams come true, like the protagonist in a movie, striving against all odds.

In a world where balance is often heralded as the ultimate goal, I discovered a deeper truth. Achieving balance in every aspect of our lives is a noble aspiration, but it's not always the path to greatness. There are times when balance must be sacrificed, when the scales must tip towards extraordinary effort to achieve extraordinary results. There will be days, weeks, even months when above-average work is required to reach those peaks of excellence, to turn dreams into reality.

Growing up, I always felt I was just one step behind everyone else. There was no special talent that set me apart. In fact, I often had to put in twice the effort just to keep up, as if I were trying to run a race with weights on my ankles. I remember countless nights of frustration, wondering if I would ever find my place, my unique spark. Then, one day, everything changed. I stumbled upon a quote that resonated deep within me: 'Everybody is a genius. But if you judge a fish by its ability to climb a tree, it will live its whole life believing that it is stupid.' Those words pierced through my self-doubt like a ray of light. I realised I had been judging myself by standards that were never meant for me. My talent wasn't missing – it just hadn't been discovered yet.

From that moment on, I embarked on a journey of exploration. I threw myself into every opportunity I could find, volunteering, trying my hand at new skills, pushing my boundaries. I was like a wanderer in a vast forest, searching for that one path that would lead me to my true self. It wasn't easy, and there were times I felt lost, but I kept going. And then, slowly but surely, I began to uncover my strengths. Each new experience was a piece of the puzzle, revealing a little more of the picture. I learned that we all have our own unique talents, but they don't always fit into the conventional moulds we're given. Some of us are meant to swim, not climb.

Now, looking back, I see that those early struggles were a necessary part of my journey. They taught me resilience, perseverance and the importance of self-belief. We are all talented in our own ways; sometimes, we just need to find the right environment to let our talents shine.

Imposter syndrome has shown me that success isn't reserved for the naturally gifted or the inherently special. It belongs to those who are consistent, determined and hardworking. It's about showing up every day, even when doubt weighs heavy, and putting in the effort. It's about resilience, pushing through the fear and proving to yourself, time and time again, that you are capable.

In the end, it's this journey – marked by struggle, relentless pursuit and ultimate triumph – that shapes us. It's what makes the victories so profoundly meaningful, and the story of our lives so incredibly compelling.

ANNA ABESADZE

I think it's clear to see that imposter syndrome, with its suffocating self-doubt and fear of exposure, can undermine even the most accomplished individuals, stealing their confidence and stifling their potential. Yet, there is a way forward. By shifting focus to our strengths and celebrating our achievements, we can turn this struggle into a path of growth and self-discovery.

Journalling emerged as my sanctuary amidst the turbulent waters of self-doubt. Documenting each triumph and milestone created a tangible reminder of my worth and capabilities. This practice transformed self-doubt into fuel for personal growth, bolstering my confidence, clarifying my goals and guiding my journey.

Embracing imperfection became a cornerstone of my journey. I learned that setbacks are stepping stones, teaching resilience and shaping my path. Success, I realised, arises not from perfection but from perseverance and embracing the journey's challenges.

In life, our beliefs sculpt our reality. I witnessed talented individuals held back by negative thoughts, missing opportunities. Embracing positivity and committing fully to each endeavour became my creed. It's not about quick fixes but about steadfast effort and resilience. By challenging negative thoughts, we break free from the shackles of self-doubt, nurturing a deeper self-understanding and purpose.

And here's the transformative revelation; I still keep the journal, but I no longer add to it. It's not because I can't keep up or find the time. Instead, it's because I've learned to harness imposter syndrome to my advantage. The journal served its purpose, showing me that every small victory counts. Now, I carry those lessons within me, no longer needing to prove my worth on paper.

Anna is an adviser to the rector and an invited lecturer at Grigol Robakidze University and serves as the global governance coordinator at World Vision International. A former US Department of State scholar though Future Leaders Exchange Program, Anna spent an exchange year in Texas and completed her MA at Tallinn University in Estonia as an Erasmus Mundus scholar.

Anna's career has spanned continents, enriching her with diverse perspectives from Europe, Asia and the United States. After gaining invaluable international experience, she returned to her home country, Georgia, to give back and drive change through the transformative power of education.

Her dedication and exemplary work ethic have earned her prestigious accolades, including the Presidential Volunteerism Award from the White House and a nomination of 'a Host Country Hero' by the Peace Corps. She has been recognised as a GESS Award Finalist for outstanding contributions in education and named Woman Changemaker of the Year 2024 by the GISR Foundation. Anna's commitment to making a difference is evident in her relentless pursuit of national and global impact.

FROM BROWN MONKEY TO LEGALLY BROWN

FROM SPOILED LITTLE BRAT TO A FIGHTER OF THE OPPRESSED

Bernadette Alonzo Cortes

In the world of high achievers, I often felt like the proverbial 'ugly duckling'. My family was a constellation of academic and athletic stars. My sister was consistently at the top of her class, her achievements celebrated at every turn. My two brothers were known for their charisma and athletic prowess, excelling in sports and leaving a mark wherever they went. In stark contrast, I was the one who seemed to fall short, constantly overshadowed by their brilliance.

As a child, my life was confined within the walls of our home. Stricken with frequent illnesses, I spent most of my days indoors, under the watchful eye of a nanny. The world outside, filled with laughter and adventure, was a distant dream I could only glimpse through the windows. My parents, despite their good intentions, believed that keeping me indoors was for my safety. They shielded me from the physical exertions and potential dangers of outdoor play, unaware of the emotional impact this confinement would have on me.

The emotional isolation I felt during these early years was profound. While other children played and explored, I was relegated to a world of dolls and household staff. My playmates were the driver, the nanny, the cook – people who, while kind, could not fill the void of peer companionship. The depth of my loneliness was highlighted, one particular day, when I was assigned to a nanny with a disability. She relied on crutches to get around, and I, in my youthful mischief, decided to hide them while she slept.

The consequences of my actions were severe. My parents, committed to teaching me a lesson, requiring me to care for the nanny for an entire week. This period was transformative. I learned to cook, to do laundry and to understand the daily struggles faced by someone with a disability. The guilt I felt for my actions was profound, and the experience imbued me with a new-found empathy and respect. It was a pivotal moment that shaped my future values and commitment to helping those in need.

PUSHING BEYOND COMFORT ZONES

As I grew older, I became increasingly aware of my differences from my siblings. Determined to carve out my own path, I moved to Manila to pursue secondary and higher education. The bustling city was a stark contrast to the sheltered environment I had known, and it was here that I hoped to prove my worth. My parents had high expectations, and I was determined to meet them.

However, despite my best efforts, I struggled academically. I was unable to secure a place in the prestigious universities that had been the dream of my parents. Their hopes for me to become a professional pharmacist seemed increasingly distant as my academic performance fell short. The pressure to succeed was immense, and the fear of disappointing my family weighed heavily on me.

With only a few months left before university acceptance deadlines, I made the decision to pursue a degree in hotel management. This choice, driven by my passion for travel and a glamorous lifestyle, felt like a compromise. I was acutely aware of how different my path was from the professional trajectories of my siblings. My decision to enter the hotel industry was met with a mix of scepticism and hope.

My entry into the hotel industry was marked by a series of challenges. I faced difficulties in adapting to the fast-paced environment and struggled with tasks that seemed simple to others. My first significant task in a five-star hotel, cooking rice for a large number of clients, ended in disaster. I failed to turn on the rice cooker, resulting in a significant problem during service. The humiliation I felt after this failure was immense, and it forced me to confront my own inadequacies.

Despite these setbacks, I remained determined. The emotional turmoil of failing in front of my colleagues was a turning point. It spurred me to work harder and to seek opportunities for growth. I knew that to overcome my past failures, I needed to push beyond my comfort zone and embrace new challenges.

TURNING LIFE AROUND IN AMERICA

When an opportunity arose to work as a chef in the United States, I saw it as a chance to reinvent myself. My family's encouragement and belief in my potential provided a crucial source of strength and hope. They believed in my ability to succeed despite my previous failures, and their support gave me the confidence to pursue this new opportunity.

My initial months in America were a whirlwind of emotions. I was excited to explore a new country and to take on new responsibilities. I had the rare opportunity to work as both a chef and a receptionist in a fine dining restaurant, a combination of roles that was unusual for a Filipino worker. This experience allowed me to confront my fear of communication and to interact with people from diverse backgrounds.

However, beneath the surface of this success, I faced significant personal challenges. I was ill-prepared for independent living and struggled with everyday tasks like using a washing machine and managing finances. The emotional strain of adjusting to a new country, combined with the loneliness of living far from home, was overwhelming.

The situation became more complicated when I fell prey to a manipulative individual who stole my money and passport, leaving me undocumented and vulnerable. The emotional toll of being exploited and facing domestic violence was profound. I felt trapped and powerless, and the trauma of these experiences was a heavy burden.

My parents' intervention was a lifeline during this dark period. They flew to the United States to rescue me, offering support and love when I needed it most. Seeing my father's reaction upon finding me – battered, traumatised and struggling – was heart-wrenching. His words of regret and determination to help me rebuild my life were a powerful motivator. The love and support from my family were crucial in helping me find the strength to move forward.

EMBRACING NEW OPPORTUNITIES

Upon returning to the Philippines, my parents encouraged me to pursue further education abroad, despite initial doubts from others. They believed in my potential to overcome my past trauma and transform my life through academic achievement. I agreed to pursue a master's degree, an ambitious step given my previous academic struggles.

My dad asked me to focus and *be the person I am destined to be* – a changemaker and a community giver. On the day of my departure for travel to Australia, my dad did not drop me at the airport because he just wanted to keep the happy, beautiful and determined persona of mine in his mind.

The initial months in Australia were tough. I struggled with academic challenges and cultural adjustments, feeling like an outsider in a another country. The communication barriers and the difference in academic expectations were daunting. My father's unwavering encouragement and belief in my abilities were a constant source of strength. His support helped me navigate these challenges and persevere through the difficulties.

The emotional weight of my father's passing, shortly after my graduation, was profound. His support and dreams for my future had been a cornerstone of my journey. His final words, urging me to honour his memory by supporting the community and achieving greatness, became a guiding principle. The promise I made to him filled me with a deep sense of responsibility and determination.

WOMEN LIVING FEARLESSLY

OVERCOMING PROFESSIONAL CHALLENGES
As I began my career in the hotel industry, I faced numerous challenges. Discrimination and prejudice were persistent issues, testing my resilience and determination. The Black Christmas of 2015, when bushfires ravaged the area, was a particularly trying time. Despite the chaos and danger, I remained committed to serving those in need, which led from one promotion to another.

During this period, my mother's declining health added another layer of emotional strain. Her wish for me to become a lawyer, following in the footsteps of our family's legacy, became a powerful motivation. Her belief in my potential to make a difference was a driving force as I considered a career change.

Little did I know, that my destiny to be a lawyer is coming to life. Her words of encouragement when she was still alive became a reality. I then studied law, breaking the stigma of a matured student.

FAILURE IS NOT AN OPTION
I felt I hit rock bottom after my multiple failures. I drove to another state where a friend whom I had mentored before offered me a waitressing job. That was the only option at the time. As lost as I was, I still managed to pass another application for law.

This time, I made sure I would ace every subject or be on top of it. It was tough, as I didn't have any form of support. I was financially broke and had no permanent house. But the failure I felt motivated me to keep on pushing.

No computer, no books and no money to go to class and work; I often would call in sick and would only return to work after I received my pay. My colleagues from the hotel got to know the situation. One exceptional colleague allocated her tips for my petrol, and the other Filipino workers would bring me food and some business clothes, so I could look like a lawyer.

I was then offered another job in the hotel, with someone I had also previously mentored. From having no job to having multiple jobs, I said to myself that, *I will be grateful and make sure I will not let them down.*

I started getting the grades, and with one high distinction after another, I earned an honours degree, and an award, sponsored by Thomson Reuters, for garnering the highest grade in commercial law during my time in university.

Then came the pandemic. We were given limited shifts, but I prayed to God that I only wanted to be safe and promised that I would help others get through the pandemic. At that time, our hotel was chosen to be a quarantine hotel, and we were lucky enough to get good benefits from the government.

I saw how the pandemic hit the mental health of people, and as a response, I used my extra money to give groceries to a hundred people. This then created a ripple effect, and some of my friends started donating too. I accidentally created a name in the community and charitable organisations asked me to join them.

FROM ORDINARY TO A SUPERHERO

I kept my promise that I would continue to support the community. I worked three jobs, studied, and in my spare time, I volunteered with Gawad Kalinga, supporting the vulnerable in the community. My name spread like fire for my advocacy, and I was given several awards within our community. I gave speeches and was called Darna (Filipino Superhero).

But it was just the beginning; international students were victimised, and women were battered. I advocated for them by reaching out to my contacts and practicing my training. This elevated me from other community leaders, and at one point, a social organiser called me during his dying hours, asking me to take care of the Filipino community.

Then came my graduation. I was excited because I wanted to practice in my chosen career, not knowing that getting into the legal industry was tough.

FROM DARNA TO BROWN MONKEY
I was the only woman of colour in the firm when the senior lawyer was asked to supervise my job. Instead of supervising me, he would humiliate me every day.

There was a time when we had to send a brief to the Court for an upcoming hearing. He started shouting at me in front of a client, even questioning why a 'monkey' was working as a lawyer. He implied that the government *milked* international students, allowing *dumb* people to study law. He obviously didn't take note of my achievements.

As a choir member, I often go to church, and on Good Friday, I attended the Seven Last Words service, ready to quit my profession and accept defeat. It was then that my musical director approached me and prayed for me. I shared my struggles with her, and she assured me it was just a test, encouraging me not to quit. She believed I was destined to become a lawyer; a dream my parents always had for me. Remarkably, everyone I met seemed to call me Attorney Cortes, reinforcing this belief. I lifted everything to God.

The emotional impact of the treatment I received was profound, but an unexpected intervention by my principal brought a turning point. The principal's swift action against the senior lawyer's misconduct was a validation of my worth and a testament to the values of the firm. This moment reinforced the importance of integrity and justice, not just in the courtroom, but in the workplace as well.

LEGALLY BROWN: THE FEARLESS ADVOCATE
Through every challenge, from familial expectations to personal trials, I've persevered. My journey from being labelled an 'ugly duckling' to becoming a respected lawyer is a testament to my resilience, hard work

and the unwavering support of my loved ones. As I continue to make my mark in the legal world, I honour my parent's legacy and strive to fulfil their dreams for me, serving as an inspiration to others and a beacon of hope.

Now with two years practising as a supervised lawyer, I have attracted different types of cases, from a woman accused of raping her partner and his friends, to a single mother who nearly lost her livelihood due to wrongful advice. I have almost seen it all. Each case has been a learning experience, a testament to the complexities of human nature, and a reminder of why I chose this path.

FULFILLING MY PARENT'S WISHES

As I look back and reflect on my life, I am filled with a deep sense of gratitude for the journey that has brought me to this point. I wish I could show my parents I have made it, to see the pride in their eyes. But I remind myself and my family that every challenge I faced was necessary, to be my torch and my compass, in fulfilling their vision for me. Each trial I encountered made me more resilient and focused, shaping both my legal profession and my personal life.

At the time of printing this book, I am thrilled to announce the establishment of my very own practice, CORTES LAWYERS, adding to my existing business EDUQUER International. This professional milestone marks the culmination of years of hard work, dedication and unwavering perseverance.

In my personal life, I am blessed to have found a passionate and loving partner who cherishes me for who I am. As I prepare to walk down the aisle, I embrace the joy and responsibility of my new role as a wife and, as a mother.

This new chapter is a testament to the power of perseverance, resilience and the unyielding belief that we can turn our dreams into reality, no matter the obstacles we face. It is a celebration of the strength that comes from overcoming adversity and the fulfilment of dreams nurtured by love, hard work and unwavering support. My story is one of hope and inspiration, proving that with determination and faith, we can achieve greatness and honour the dreams of those who believe in us.

Bernadette Alonzo Cortes, an Australian legal practitioner, stands as a beacon of resilience, determination and unwavering dedication. Currently the CEO of Eduquer International and on the brink of opening her own practice, Cortes Lawyers, Bernadette's journey is nothing short of inspirational.

Born in the Philippines, Bernadette moved to the United States in her early twenties. After enduring a tragic event overseas, her faith and her parent's emotional support became the cornerstone of her recovery. Determined to rebuild her life, she sought higher education in Australia. The values and lessons she learned there not only paved the way for her Australian citizenship but also ignited her passion for law. As a manager of a hotel, her empathetic nature and ability to connect deeply with her staff revealed her true calling – to become a lawyer.

Pursuing her legal studies at Victoria University, Bernadette graduated with a bachelor of laws (graduate entry) honours. Her academic journey was marked by excellence, competing in moots and achieving the highest grades in commercial law. She was mentored by a Supreme Court Justice and gained invaluable experience by shadowing Kings Counsel and international barristers, shaping her into a formidable legal mind.

As a woman of colour from a country where English is a second language, Bernadette faced relentless discrimination. Yet, she emerged victorious, proving that barriers are meant to be broken. Her journey from adversity to triumph has earned her recognition as a community leader and a finalist in the Women Changing the World awards.

Known for her unyielding grit and compassion, Bernadette

transformed her life from being penniless to owning multiple companies. She intimately understands the journey from debt to security, hope and opportunity. Every case she handles is a testament to her personal touch, from initial consultation to resolution. She transforms traditional legal practice by eschewing jargon and maintaining an open line of communication with her clients.

Bernadette's commitment to change extends beyond her professional life. She is dedicated to transforming lives, one at a time, and inspiring others to rise above life's adversities. Despite her numerous business ventures, she remains deeply connected to the community, offering legal support to those who need it most. She is a relentless advocate for education, financial stability and equal opportunities for people of colour. Her work with Gawad Kalinga, supporting domestic violence victims, highlights her relentless drive to empower the vulnerable.

A mother and soon-to-be wife, Bernadette envisions a future filled with love, support and shared dreams with the person who has guided her journey. While she is a tenacious advocate in her professional life, her friends cherish her as a cheerful and playful soul outside of work.

Bernadette Alonzo Cortes is not just a lawyer; she is a symbol of hope and perseverance. Her story inspires us all to believe that no matter the obstacles, we can rise, excel and make a lasting impact on the world. Her unwavering dedication and transformative journey remind us that with determination and compassion, we can overcome any challenge and achieve greatness.

SURVIVOR NOT VICTIM

Bethany Chambers

Gen X may be a micro-generation, but we are well known to be tough, resourceful and resilient – skills that I've had to depend on more than some. Squished between the boomers and the millennials, we didn't grow up with mobile phones or social media, that was to come later. What we did have were parents who forgot we existed and the unbridled freedom to *'be home before the streetlights come on'*. I didn't have a great childhood; a broken home and a mother who regularly reminded me I was an unloved mistake. Nothing was ever good enough. I was never good enough. Welcome the overachiever and people-pleaser – survival attributes learnt early in life.

The great Bob Marley offered many words of wisdom including, 'You never know how strong you are until being strong is your only choice.' I'm one of those lucky(?) people, who, if there is even a 0.03% chance of complications or something going wrong, I'm your woman – where do I sign?

Homelessness at thirteen was 'character building', but at least I was free from the psychological abuse, traumatically replaced with sexual and domestic violence – a child in an adult world. Community initiatives provided me with safe affordable housing in a different part of Melbourne, away from the pressures of survival and the drug dealer role models. Away from any likelihood of running unexpectantly into *Mother*, who somehow still held a grasp upon me.

Often, overlooked choices are there every day; forks in the road, decisions to be made, an understanding that there will be a ripple effect. The destination may not be visible, however, the alternatives are stark; drug abuse and prostitution as a means to survive, versus the ability to be a contributing member of society, a new beginning. My survivor, rather than victim, mindset gave me the desire to grasp ALL the opportunities that came my way, excited to experience everything I had missed. Within a short period of time I was settled into my little unit, enjoying the safety of lockable doors, the ability to feed myself and save money by cooking, rather than relying on takeaway food. There aren't stoves on the street nor a fridge, unless you count the outside temperature during a Melbourne winter. The convenience and ability to access and use a bathroom at any time of night, without concern of the council locking it, was a luxury and privilege previously unattainable.

With little assistance, soon I was juggling two jobs and returning service back to the community through volunteering. Here I found friendship, kindness, a sense of belonging and, importantly, a purpose. Volunteers, and those who give freely to others, are a special type of person; volunteering embraces and encourages kindness in their very being. Soon enough a member of my St John Ambulance unit became aware that I had recently moved into my one-bedroom level brick unit with the absolute bare basics. What's wrong with two milk crates and a couple of fence palings being used as a bookcase?

Before long there came a knock at my door, where stood my fellow volunteers, as well as an odds and bods collection of second-hand furniture to help me create a home. There was everything from a bed frame and two-seater couch to a coffee table and a collection of tea, coffee and matching sugar jars, already filled. This gesture of kindness would leave an ever-lasting impression upon me, along with a certain understanding that I would never again have to be alone, me against the world. But if ever there was a time where my back was against the wall, I would not surrender, but be guided by my moral compass and inner warrior.

Perhaps it was the camaraderie or the desire to have a greater impact, but I joined the Queensland Police Service after decades working in the banking and recruitment sectors. My timing was perfect, as shortly thereafter the sector imploded with the Global Financial Crisis. I was a general duties officer, which meant shift work, lights and sirens, a collection of PTSD moments and a sense of mateship like no other. Being a police officer is so much more than an occupation; it becomes a part of your existence, your being, your identity.

Life was great. I had married my soulmate, Scott, who shared my passion for helping others through volunteering with the State Emergency Service, where we met. We completed our blended family of my two boys with the arrival of our daughter, Calista. Of course, pregnancy was anything but routine, finding myself hospitalised from five months pregnant until Calista's emergency caesarean birth at thirty-two weeks. This is where we first encountered Alexis, when I found myself unable to walk due to the weight of a growing baby and my body's over-production of *relaxin* – a hormone that loosens the muscles, joints and ligaments during pregnancy. Then there was the excruciating heartache of having to leave our baby, first in NICU, followed by neonatal for a month. Even during this time, when my baby's life was in the balance, Alexis would demand my unwelcomed attention.

During my pregnancy, I'd also developed a *spigelian hernia;* the rarest of hernias. This type of hernia occurs through a previous surgical scar or abdominal trauma. Mine developed where my appendix was removed some twelve years earlier, whilst twenty weeks pregnant with my eldest son. Thankfully, he was unharmed, but recovery had been long, painful and lengthy due to pregnancy.

Fast-forward eighteen months, we had bought our forever home and were settled in as a family. In all respects, we were thriving. I was in my element as a senior constable and finalist for Queensland Police Officer of the Year. My involvement with a youth engagement program, my career planning and development plan, were all well underway. I was eight years into my career when everything turned upside-down.

It was a warm sunny day, when I was attending police taser training in a group which was quite dynamic and physical. Throughout the day, I started experiencing a stabbing pain in my abdomen, which came and went, but was powerful enough to have me catch my breath and grasp my stomach. As the pain became more frequent and severe, I was sent home from training early, but I didn't get too far before the ripping of my stomach muscles made it impossible to drive. Struggling to breathe, and with tears running down my face, I called Scott. An ambulance met me at the side of the road, doubled over in pain unable to speak or walk, the green whistle, a strong pain relief administered by paramedics, did little to alleviate the ripping, stabbing, all-encompassing pain.

Despite my condition, hernias are deemed non-life threatening, so I was placed onto the elective surgery list for an operation in 'two days' time' – my birthday. I was advised that the hernia mesh, polypropylene (think a mesh bag of oranges – it's very similar with a finer weave), designed to support tissue around a hernia, would be implanted via laparoscopic surgery. This surgery comprises of three incisions in a triangle pattern made for surgical instruments and implanting the mesh, which is then secured by tacks. Once the mesh is in situ, tissue grows over, reinforcing the repair over time. Lesions and adhesions to other organs can also occur. Hernia repairs are deemed a low-risk operation, with over twenty million surgeries performed annually worldwide. Complications hadn't even been mentioned, despite mesh being a permanent, implanted foreign body, and it was expected to last a lifetime. Wheeled into theatre, I was anticipating a few weeks of healing time ... and then back to my almost fairytale existence.

Many hours later, in my bland hospital room, securely enveloped within stiff white sheets, I was on the phone to the family, feeling groggy, but figuring it was the anaesthetic. Then, unexpectedly, I stop responding. I awake, confused, struggling to focus, as I'm in a wheeled bed, steel sidebars firmly in place, being rushed through brightly lit corridors, the smell distinctly clinical. Surrounded by people in blue surgical gowns, I see my husband, Scott, fear etched on his face, racing alongside. I distinctly recall telling him to contact my dad, as well as his best friend, Shane. I didn't want him to be alone through whatever was happening. Before I can process any response, darkness again envelopes me.

ICU machines competing for attention, a breathing tube filling my throat, I frantically scour this foreign environment for anything familiar. Heart pounding, reflected with a mechanical echo, eyes finally lock on Scott, tired and strained, seated protectively by my side. The screens reflected in his eyes, as tears of relief silently weave down his face registering that I am awake. Patiently and gently, he explains the operation, well, the first one that day, had gone wrong, *terribly wrong*. Lesions from the previous hernia repair eighteen months earlier had been cut internally, causing horrific blood loss … and my death.

In order to gain emergency access to my abdominal cavity, surgeons performed a laparotomy. I was cut from my ribs to groin, where over two litres of blood had pooled, sealed with forty-two external staples. Life would never be the same again.

In the short time that I was in surgery, permanent damage had occurred. Pain engulfed me as I struggled to focus and take in what Scott is saying, including that I was no longer on a ward but a private room, in ICU. Pain meds, shock and the reassurance of Scott's touch meant blessed sleep soon took over. It was a difficult night, despite the use of a morphine pump as I hurt everywhere, including my bruised ribs after enduring CPR. If I'd been told I had been hit by a truck, it wouldn't have surprised me.

My throat is scratched, dry and sore after the removal of my breathing tube, my voice a whisper. 'What now?' I ask the white-coated doctor who materialised the following morning. Due to the severity of my condition, I was to stay in hospital with a central line in place for fear of further complications. A central line is a short-term catheter inserted into the jugular vein in the neck. My already low blood pressure was a factor too, especially with the morphine pump required for pain control (which happened to be a critical factor leading to my clinical death following further surgery later that same year).

Remarkably, a week after being collected roadside by the ambulance, I was discharged and homeward bound. The prognosis was positive in that I was healing, and although in a lot of pain, would make a full recovery and return to duty within the next six to eight weeks. How wrong they were.

Weeks and then months went by, while the pain in my abdomen persisted. I now had a suite of specialists, but they weren't talking about full recovery anymore; the language had changed, as had my situation. I wasn't able to work, and the bills were starting to grow, as we had become a one-income family, with chronic illness and all the additional expenses that go with that: medical appointments, physiotherapist, psychiatrists and the pharmaceuticals. Having previously hit rock bottom, there was *no way* this survivor was going back to the streets – I had my fairytale to return to.

Pain is the body's way of signalling to the brain that something has happened suddenly and intensely, requiring immediate attention. Chronic pain, however, is categorised as pain which lasts longer than six months and continues once the injury or illness has been treated. I had fallen into the 12-30% who experience hernia mesh complications, including a smaller substrate who also developed autoimmune conditions. I wasn't ready. No two ways about it; I was not accepting that this pain would be with me forever more. I wasn't accepting that my world, which was so full of promise, had changed so dramatically.

Our family dynamic had changed with the arrival of Alexis. Alexis' role was to break me by any means. She was relentless; deep sleep was a distant memory as she woke me violently and painfully every few hours, demanding attention. Most mornings, Scott awakes as the night sky is lightening with the promise of dawn to find me rocking through the excruciating pain, exacerbated by hours of full-body spasms. I became a zombie, continually tortured with pain, exhaustion and a growing medication list as I was ping-ponged from one specialist to another, riding a roller-coaster of hope and promise of recovery. Instead, I was met with a plethora of side effects, while still trying my best to parent our three children. They needed me, still young and far from independent, I too, desperately needed them.

Alexis' torment wasn't merely physical, she also owned my psyche. Grieving the loss of my career, the strong capable and confident woman I once was became a distant memory. Every siren a tolling bell, constant reminders of my former much-loved self. As the messages of *get well soon* lose significance, the invitations stop coming, it's this moment that Alexis shares her slideshow. A barrage of images invade my mind. Death in varying forms, picture after picture, the young, the old, the murdered, scared and broken. Different positions and poses all with a sad story attached; I know because I was involved with them all.

Depression and anxiety are partners when experiencing such a loss of independence, and with pain a constant companion, physical exhaustion invaded every facet of my existence. Constantly questioning which is worse; to have had an active, involved parent who can no longer kick a ball or go for a bike ride or never having the ability to share in those activities, memories unable to be created. I sobbed for my children and the mother they had lost, the mother they would never know. Alexis always knew how to torment me, she relentlessly repeated, whispering softly, *The truth is, you are a burden, an unnecessary complication in these good people's lives. They certainly didn't sign up for an invalid or to be a carer.* Rather than being the glue holding the family together, I became the reason we couldn't go to theme parks and were at risk of losing our home. They deserved better. Alexis wore me down. I begged Scott to let me go, so he could find a partner worthy of his love and devotion; he deserved an able-bodied wife. Stubbornly, he refused to let me to push him away, repeatedly reassuring me that I was loved, an integral part of the family. Scott's words of wisdom: 'We don't have problems, we have challenges, as challenges can be overcome.' From this as a family we would design and adapt into what is referred to as our 'new normal'.

So many things previously taken for granted, like not having to rest between unpacking and packing the dishwasher or being unable to lift our two-year-old, even sweeping the floors was an impossibility. A pamper at the hairdresser's a distant memory, as being in any position for an extended time wasn't possible, due to pain flares. These occur without warning, often lasting hours or even days. During this time, I was averaging eight ambulance trips a year to hospital with uncontrollable pain. My beautiful children experiencing the trauma of watching a loved one, incapacitated with pain, powerless to help. How can I keep putting them through this? Breathing deeply, I repeat like a mantra, 'I'm a survivor, not a victim, this too shall pass,' as I am transported to hospital yet again.

I became empowered by the need and requirement to parent – despite Alexis' insistence to pull the covers over my head and ignore the school alarm, to give in to that all-consuming darkness of depression, a form of paralysis. It's a cold winter's morning and the desire to succumb is powerful. My gaze falls upon my left wrist, to a small tattoo; *This too shall pass.* I throw back the covers in defiance of Alexis, knowing that broken or not, my family needed me and WE, together, would survive – one day at a time. Forks in the road, my decision readily made, to become a present parent and person in the lives of my children and family. Instead of merely existing, it was time to overcome and adapt.

Alexis is ever present, after all she is me, Alexis is my body. She is also my abuser from whom there is no escape. Every day now is a battle for me, as I manoeuvre through a world filled with constant pain and a plethora of pills, but at least I'm mostly functioning. It depends upon the doctor as to the cause, the diagnosis; numerous autoimmune diseases including fibromyalgia, nerve damage and associated pain in my abdomen, right groin and entirety of my right leg. Due to an unknown cause my three lower ribs now sit on top of my hips, continually grating.

Despite a further thirty-plus surgeries and procedures, with an unfair advantage of accruing complications, I am here, *alive*. A present parent and loving wife, mostly on my terms and importantly have again found my purpose. I designed my own social enterprise, Merry Go Round Toys. This venture I've created is a meaningful and purposeful way in which I can work within my limitations whilst doing what I love – being a survivor not a victim; empowering others on their journeys.

BETHANY CHAMBERS

I have had a very tumultuous life commencing when my mother and stepfather absconded with me interstate at nine years old. My father, unawares, attended my piano lesson for his scheduled time with me, only to be informed I wasn't there. I experienced homelessness as a young teenager, on the streets of Melbourne, enduring assault and the need to steal to survive. I was lost, until community assistance found me accommodation and gave me options. I repaid this with years of volunteering until I later fought hard for my dream career as a police officer, with a strong focus with disengaged youth. After eight years of service, a routine hernia repair operation changed my life forever.

My medical journey has been a veritable roller-coaster where I have endured over twenty-eight procedures with a myriad of complications. The repercussions are that I now live in constant pain with numerous chronic illnesses including fibromyalgia as well as a physical disability, every day is a battle against my body. The loss of my career, the strong capable and confident woman I once was, a distant memory.

Adjustment took time, as did gaining some semblance of management of my many chronic conditions, which continue to impact my day-to-day life. I have had three hernia mesh implants within my abdomen which have caused permanent nerve damage. With chronic pain as my constant companion, there was no surprise that I would struggle with my mental health as well. I felt that I was a burden, an unnecessary complication in the lives of the ones I loved. With help, I learnt that this was a time and type of grieving, what had been lost was monumental and what our new 'normal' landscape depicted now so different. Throughout this time of adjustment and understanding of my health, despite the reality of it declining, I started toying with an idea.

Merry Go Round Toys was born in 2023, despite me having our logo commissioned five years previously, the timing was now ripe. Merry Go Round Toys keeps developmental tools accessible and affordable, counteracting the troubling trend of such items becoming luxury goods. Our approach efficiently capitalises on the circular economy concept, where products are given new life, and buyers are assured of items' completeness and condition without harmful chemical usage. Presently no-one else is addressing the fact that 80% of preloved children's toys end up in our landfill, oceans or incinerated. To be replaced with poor-quality cheaply made items which only compound the issue with their manufacture and over-supply.

Merry Go Round Toys is more than just a toy retailer but a business underpinned with a strong ethos partnering with organisations like Redland Bay Men's Shed, Share the Dignity and Houses of Hope program. With the inclusion of toy packs for children in vulnerable housing situations, volunteering and monetary donations, we have ambitiously elevated our role from a mere retailer to a key supporter of our community's wellbeing.

This self-devised social enterprise has adopted a strong stance and ethos of support for our environment with a social focus. We are blessed to have a variety of supporters who actively donate toys straight to Merry Go Round Toys. As we don't have a consignor to share the proceeds with, part proceeds are returned to Bayside Salvation Army or Share the Dignity in the form of a donation. We also work closely with our men's shed whom provide quality toy repairs and beautiful handmade items for us to resell.

Merry Go Round Toys, although only just in our second year, have gained a dedicated following and attention. I was a finalist for a 2023 Chamber of Commerce Business Excellence Award and managed to clinch the coveted Business Excellence Award for Innovation and Sustainability. In 2024 we exploded onto the global stage with a Global Recognition Award for our innovative approach to sustainable retail in the children's toy market. In addition, the prestigious and coveted Women Changing the World GOLD award for social enterprise, along with AusMumpreneur awards in the regions of Social Enterprise and Disabled Business Excellence. I am being recognised as a passionate and focused speaker and proud disabled advocate of resilience coupled with compassion.

Instagram: instagram.com/merrygoroundtoys?igsh=MW5ocTlhbWZ-rZ2pz&utm_sourc e=qr
Facebook: facebook.com/amerrygoround.com.au
LinkedIn: linkedin.com/in/bethany-chambers- 00b17766?utm_source=share&utm_campaign=share_via&utm_content=profile&utm_medium=ios_app
Website: merrygoroundtoys.com.au

SIGNIFICANTLY SEEN

EMPOWERING SELF AND OTHERS

Dr Dale Laing-Hall

There I was, in a boardroom that felt cold and empty, sitting in a chair surrounded by six directors and VPs for the very first time. The room was sterile, the walls a drab shade of beige and the air was thick with tension. My emotions were high. My heart was beating so hard, you could hear it from across the table, my hands were sweating and I felt utterly out of place. The taste in my mouth suddenly vanished, replaced by the bitter tang of anxiety.

You see, at one point, I was that fearful of speaking to people in power – professionals with titles like manager, director or executive. My self-esteem was low. I didn't believe I was worth anyone's time. I lacked confidence and felt powerless to have anyone listen to me. It wasn't just about being in the presence of these high-ranking officials, it was a deep-seated belief that I didn't belong.

A JOURNEY OF SELF-DOUBT

Growing up, I was often told to be quiet, to speak only when spoken to. My family believed in traditional values where children were seen, not heard. I internalised this message deeply. In high school, hurtful comments about my appearance made me question my worth. 'I could never be with someone like you,' my crush said. 'Your hair is too short and ugly, and your skin is way too black.' Those words cut deeper than any physical wound.

In the workplace, I was advised to stop smiling in order to be taken seriously. Each instance chipped away at my self-worth, reinforcing the narrative that *I was not enough*. I apologised profusely for mistakes that weren't my fault, kept quiet when I didn't agree, nodded and smiled, and simply did what I was told. I became a master at 'sucking it up'. I didn't know there was another way. I didn't know I wasn't loving myself.

My mother taught us well; to be kind, respectful, always give and help others. But somewhere along the way, I missed the lesson on being kind to myself, respecting myself, giving and loving myself *first*. If you know what I mean, then you understand very well what it is to *not be seen*, to be dismissed before you even get a chance to cast your vote.

A TURNING POINT

One day, during a personal family disagreement, I found myself at a McDonald's restaurant. I saw a girl, sad and crying, waiting for a ride that never came. In that moment, I realised the power of small acts of kindness and the opportunity we all have to make a difference in someone's life. That encounter was a turning point for me. I saw a reflection of my own struggles in her tears and understood the profound impact of empathy and kindness.

It was imperative for me to see myself, to change the narrative and decide who I really wanted to be. I spent nights crying, staring into the ocean, journalling, attending numerous free and paid trainings, courses, counselling sessions and taking myself on walks. I was rediscovering, reconnecting, tearing down and rebuilding myself. I knew I had to reach deep within and embrace that *I was completely and totally worth it*. I had earned my spot around that table and any other table I deemed my next – just like everyone else.

EMBRACING EMOTIONAL INTELLIGENCE

My journey with emotional intelligence (EQ) began when I realised that understanding and managing my emotions was crucial to my personal and professional growth. EQ is about recognising our own emotions and those of others, and using this awareness to manage our behaviour and relationships effectively. It's about being significantly seen – not just by others, but by ourselves.

In my doctoral research on emotional intelligence, I found that workplaces with people of high emotional intelligence experience increased job satisfaction, reduced turnover and enhanced productivity. The people were empathetic, understanding, caring, willing to collaborate. They were emotionally mature and able to express themselves without hurting others or themselves. These environments fostered trust and inclusion, creating spaces where everyone felt valued and seen. Why is this important? Well, in my experience, people will generally trust others who are consistently truthful, keep their promises, seek justice for all, respect others and remain accountable.

OVERCOMING CHALLENGES

One of the biggest challenges I faced was overcoming my fear of speaking up. During meetings, I would often sit quietly, even when I had valuable contributions to make. The fear of being judged, of saying something wrong or of being dismissed kept me silent. But I knew that to be seen, I had to find my voice.

I started small in intimate spaces, less intimidating settings. Gradually, I built up my confidence. I practiced mindfulness and grounding techniques to manage my anxiety. I reminded myself that my perspective was valuable, and I had a right to be heard. It was a slow and sometimes painful process, but with each small victory, I grew stronger!

A NEW NARRATIVE

John C Maxwell once said, 'To be significant, all you have to do is make a difference with others wherever you are, with whatever you have, day by day.' This idea stuck with me, because it's about finding meaning in our everyday actions.

Changing the narrative meant redefining what it meant to be successful. My late grandmother cautioned me against aiming too high due to societal limits. Years later, I realised my dream wasn't about titles, bragging, having accolades or money – it was about supporting people and creating better life experiences, especially for those who were overlooked or treated unfairly, as I was. It was about being significantly seen and helping others to be seen as well.

LIVING FEARLESSLY

Living fearlessly means stepping out of the shadows and into the light. It means embracing your true self and allowing yourself to be seen. It means standing up for yourself and others, even when it's difficult. It means being kind to yourself, respecting yourself and loving yourself first.

If you've ever felt *meant for more*, now is your time to move beyond being noticed to being truly seen and significant. Let's create environments defined by empathy, kindness and positive actions. To be significantly seen, we need the acronym REPORTS:

R: Recognise and Acknowledge: Appreciate others' efforts. A simple 'thank you' can go a long way.

E: Empathy: Understand others' perspectives and respond with kindness.

P: Presence: Engage fully in conversations. Focus on the person in front of you.

O: Offer Support: Make it a point to assist others.

R: Reflect and Improve: Reflect on your actions and seek feedback.

T: Trust and Inclusion: Promote diversity, ensuring everyone feels appreciated.

S: Self-Awareness and Emotional Intelligence: Develop these skills; they can transform your life.

THE IMPACT OF EMOTIONAL INTELLIGENCE

My doctoral research on EQ showed that workplaces with high emotional intelligence boost the true meaning of belonging, where every individual feels valued, included and connected to themselves, their peers and the organisation's mission and goals. It goes beyond diversity and inclusion by ensuring that people not only have a seat at the table, but also feel they genuinely belong and can contribute their best selves. These findings were not just statistics to me, they were a validation of my journey and my experiences. They reinforced the importance of emotional intelligence in creating positive, inclusive environments.

MOVING FORWARD

Today, I'm not the same person who once sat silently in that cold, empty boardroom. I have learned to speak up, to stand tall and to claim my space. I have learned that my voice matters and I have the power to make a difference. I have embraced my journey with emotional intelligence and used it to create spaces where everyone else around me feels valued and seen. I saw myself in that girl in McDonald's, so I reached out, gave her a ride and sent her off with a hug, reminding her that she is not alone and no matter what took place *today*, a better *tomorrow* is coming.

Living fearlessly is not about being without fear, it's about moving forward despite the fear. It's about trusting yourself and believing in your worth. It's about being significantly seen, not just by others, but by yourself. It's about knowing that you have the power to create change and make a difference.

CONCLUSION

To be unbound is to transcend societal constraints. It means breaking free from the chains of self-doubt and external limitations. It means empowering ourselves and others to be valued, heard and respected. True leadership is about empowering others to be significantly seen, heard and valued in every endeavour. This chapter of my life is a testament to the power of emotional intelligence and the importance of being significantly seen. It's a story of overcoming fear, embracing self-worth and creating a positive impact. It's a journey of living fearlessly and helping others to do the same.

Thank you for joining me on this journey. Let's continue to create a world where everyone feels significantly seen and valued, where empathy and positive actions lead to thriving lives.

Let's live fearlessly and make a difference – one act of kindness at a time!

DR DALE LAING-HALL

Dr Dale Laing-Hall, DBA, MS-HRM, is an Afro-Latina born and raised in Roatan, Honduras, she is the last of seven children, considered the favourite child of her mother, Miriam, and wife to her high school friend in IT Jabnel.

Dr Dale is an executive human resources consultant, transformational thought leader and an emotional intelligence leader who is on a mission to bridge the employee-employer gap and positively impact workplaces and home spaces.

Dr Dale empowers professionals to master emotional intelligence to strengthen and cultivate strong relationships, communicate effectively, overcome challenges and empathise with others.

Dr Dale holds a master's degree in human resource management and a bachelor's degree in health service administration, in addition, last year she completed her doctorate degree in business administration with a specialisation in social impact management which allowed her to focus her research on the concept of emotional intelligence (EQ) and its effects on employees in the workplace.

Powered with all of this knowledge, experience and passion, she has embarked on a new journey of starting her very own leadership development/coaching and consulting company called Dale Reports, LLC supporting professionals, HR pros and business owners. Because of her invaluable relationships with people throughout her education, work life and lived experiences, she is prepared with all the necessary tools to aid leaders in fostering a thriving culture effectively and strategically to empower their most valuable assets – human beings!

DR DALE LAING-HALL

Lastly, coupled with her coaching, training and career endeavours, Dale volunteers at Feeding South Florida, Human Resource Association of Broward County (HRABC) as the chair of professional development, board member of Roatan Women Association Non-Profit, and gives back to business leaders and HR professionals by promoting empathy and self-awareness in each connection. All while sharing her knowledgeable perspective on podcasts, businesses, universities, summits and workshops.

BE BOLD, LIVE FEARLESSLY

Ellie D Shefi

'It is in the moments of decision that your destiny is shaped.'
Tony Robbins

Right or left?
Stay or go?
Do I, or don't I?
What if I choose unwisely?

Each of us has faced tough decisions and made choices that altered our lives. Decisions are scary because they have the power to change everything. And the power to maintain the status quo. Do you make your decisions boldly? Or does fear paralyse you until you are inert – living on autopilot?

I lived on autopilot for years. I behaved in the way others expected. I did what they demanded. I even mindlessly ate what they placed before me. I made no conscious decisions, and I lived a robotic life utterly void of authenticity, abundance and joy. Why? Because I was paralysed by fear – fear of rejection; fear of failure; fear of mental, emotional and physical pain.

I relinquished all control of my life and let my circumstances dictate my existence. You see, I'm an abuse survivor, rape survivor and domestic violence survivor, who has lived in hiding under a fake name. I've struggled financially, lived in my car and asked restaurants for the food they were throwing away at the end of the night. I'm a cancer survivor and medical miracle who's had thirteen major surgeries and been defying the doctors' death deadlines for more than twenty years.

And yet, despite those events and circumstances, I've learned to take back control over my life, boldly make intentional decisions from a place of fearlessness, harness my power and create a life I love! I may have been forged by fire, but I am free by design.

Through five decades of getting back up every time life has knocked me down, I've learned to live life on my terms and decide who I want to be and how I want to show up in the world. Now, I unapologetically stand in my power and use my voice to empower others. I'm an attorney, advisor, advocate, coach, consultant, keynote speaker, strategist, multiple number-one international bestselling and award-winning author, publisher, philanthropist, podcast and TV host, a two-time discrimination and human rights lawyer of the year, a *New York Times* power lawyer, one of the most influential women leaders to watch, one of the most admired women leaders in business, one of the top entrepreneurs changing the game and the recipient of the 2024 Women Changing the World Awards in the Woman in Literature and the Woman in Media categories.

How did I navigate the lowest of lows and soar to the heights of success? Through moment after moment of facing my fear and living boldly. Everything changed for me when I embraced fear, learned to take action (even when afraid!), and began making decisions from a place of conviction – when I took control of my path, my destiny, my business, my health, my relationships, my life!

Your moments of living boldly and fearlessly are the moments that will change and shape your life. You see, your decisions fuel your actions. And it's your actions that fuel your clarity and your path forward.

In those moments when you draw a line in the sand and decide that something has to change, that something needs to be different, you start to take action. At that first moment, you probably won't be clear on the whole path and you won't have all the details. But because you've made the decision, because you've overcome the inertia stemming from fear, you're able to take one step, one action, which then leads to another step, another action, and then the path will unfold. Clarity comes from action.

WOMEN LIVING FEARLESSLY

Each of us can live boldly when we consciously, intentionally and fearlessly make decisions, as they are the foundation upon which we can build an aligned, joyful life we love.

I've had four pivotal moments of fearlessness in my life … four moments when I faced fear head on and boldly charged forward … four moments of decision that changed the trajectory of my life. I'd like to share those with you now.

CHOOSING ME

I'm a domestic violence survivor. I was friends with my ex-husband for years before we married, but the person he admired as a friend was anathema to who he needed as a spouse. He tried to mould me into his ideal wife through whatever means necessary. I initially stayed in the marriage so as to not have to face my own mother's ridicule (she had placed bets with her family on how long the marriage would last). Over time, I was broken down to merely following the path of least resistance. *If I just do what I'm told, then maybe I won't get hurt.* That fear was my life for two years. In my mind, the path of least resistance equaled survival. But it actually meant my death.

Things got bad during the summer of 2000. I was supposed to be starting my second year of law school, but, instead, I was in the hospital from the stress of living in fight-or-flight; my organs and bodily systems were failing. I had developed somatoform disorder. My body physically manifested my emotional trauma. A doctor who figured out that spousal abuse was causing my illness contacted my father and said, 'I think this is what's happening, and your daughter will be dead by Christmas.' Well, that was all my father needed to hear. He reached out to the local law enforcement and organised my rescue. I had no part in the plan. I knew the situation was dire, but I would not leave on my own. I was so debilitated that I was a shell, an automaton that simply did whatever my ex-husband instructed. My health had deteriorated to the extent that my life literally depended on the help of others to get me out. Four police officers, plus my dad, came to our apartment. Two officers pinned down my ex-husband while two took my arms and pulled me out. My dad waited in a running car, and as soon as the officers put me in the back seat, he hit the gas and drove thirty-eight hours across the country to get me to safety.

I was put into hiding and given a fake name. I became a ghost – on paper and to myself. I was placed in a home with a man I didn't know. I was terrified and would barricade the doors and windows. I barely left my room and had lost all ability to make a decision. Every single day for months, I ate the exact same thing for breakfast, lunch and dinner because no-one told me what to eat, and I was not capable of making my own decisions or functioning independently.

I spent hours each day, month after month, in intense trauma therapy. One day, my therapist challenged me to go to the grocery store on my own. My assignment was simply to buy something – anything – from the store. I couldn't do it. I ran out of the store in tears, hysterical because I couldn't decide what to buy. As I stood in the grocery store parking lot, sobbing uncontrollably and utterly broken, something shifted in me. That's when I had my first major moment of fearlessness. I finally understood that, if things were going to get better, I had to be the one to change it.

I had to be the one to decide that my life was worth more, *that I was worth more*. I had to be the one to decide I was worth living a joyful life I loved.

I had to face my fears and step into action.

Instead of seeing myself as the girl whose future had been snatched from her, I had to choose to see my situation as an opportunity. *I am complete ashes*, I told myself. *This is ground zero for my life. What an incredible opportunity I have to start over from scratch and rebuild myself into exactly who I want to be. What an amazing gift that, in starting over,*

WOMEN LIVING FEARLESSLY

I get to define for myself who I will be, what I will stand for and how I will live my life from this point forward. What freedom!

I recognised right then and there that my experiences were a blessing. I finally understood I was powerful beyond measure, and that I actually had control over my life in all aspects – even those I had thus far felt powerless to control. I realised I had the power to write my own story the way I wanted it to be ... not my ex-husband, not my parents, not society and not labels placed on me by an outside observer. *Me*. I had the power to choose. And I had the power to do anything and be anyone I desired. I had the power to create and live life on my own terms. I just had to lean in to being bold and living fearlessly.

A lot has happened in the decades since my rescue and resurrection. I've continued to design my life deliberately and with intention, based on that initial moment of fearlessness, through every obstacle life has thrown my way. Just because I decided to take control of my life once, however, doesn't mean I'm magically in this impervious, unshakable state of perpetual power and positivity. Choosing how I show up in each moment is a daily decision, a daily practice.

But, by doing this every single day, external circumstances no longer define me. The views of others no longer define me. *I define myself*.

CHOOSING MY FUTURE

I spent a year away from law school healing and rebuilding my life. After months in hiding, I moved to Europe. While there, I met five incredible women who became my sisters, and, through their love, patience, compassion and support, I came back to life. The love of this sisterhood healed me, and I built the new me from ashes. It also was the catalyst for much of the work I do now with women – helping them write and publish books, hosting events, providing strategic business and individual coaching – steadfastly guiding them to push past their fears, claim their voices and step into their power!

My life in Europe was good, and I was happy. I had learned how to function independently again. I was living, I was laughing and I was thriving.

But, according to the rules of the American Bar Association, a student had to spend at least two of their three years of law school in residence at the degree-granting institution in order to receive their Juris Doctorate from that institution ... and they had to graduate within five years of matriculating. So there came a moment when I had to decide whether to come out of hiding and finish law school, so I could graduate within the permissible time frame, or whether to remain safely and happily in Europe with my support system.

This second major moment of fearlessness – of choosing me ... of staring down my past and choosing my future – was not an easy one.

Ultimately, I decided that my ex-husband had already taken enough from me. I decided that while he had broken my spirit, taken my very identity and caused my body to shut down, I would not let him take anything else from me. I refused to let him take my dreams or my future, so *I chose me!* I chose to return to law school; I chose to triumph over fear. However, my ex-husband was still in the vicinity.

CHOOSING GRATITUDE

I got my law degree – my ticket to my future – but at the cost of my health. The stress of my ex-husband being nearby, following me and trying to contact me, caused me to live that year in perpetual fight-or-flight mode, causing prolonged trauma exposure. I got sick again. So very, very sick. I was diagnosed with adrenal tumour Cushing's syndrome and had the first few of what would be thirteen major surgeries.

From that point, I spent the better part of two decades living in and out of hospitals, fighting for my life. By 2007, I had grown tired of the pain, tired of the fear and tired of the constant struggle to survive. I was giving up. I'd had enough. I was done fighting the doctors' death deadlines. Then one day, everything changed. It was a day I had to have another excruciating test. When it was time for me to go for testing, the porter came to get me from my room and wheeled my wheelchair down hallways that he had never taken me through before.

He wheeled me through the hallways of the area in the hospital where everyone was on a ventilator, either paralysed from the neck down or in a coma. I looked into room after room and realised that any one of those patients would give anything to feel the pain I was feeling. In an instant, I realised that my pain was not something to be feared, but rather, was an incredible blessing! I recognised that I was so lucky to be able to feel pain travel around my body. I thanked God that I still had nerves that were connected and synapses that were firing as they should. What a gift! I turned my pity party into gratitude, and my weariness became resolve. I was flooded with gratitude for my body and all it provided me.

In that third major moment of fearlessness, I once again took control of my life; this time by embracing the power of gratitude.

Have you ever noticed that when you allow yourself to feel truly grateful about something, you cannot simultaneously feel fearful, angry, anxious, worried or frustrated?

Go ahead – try it. Think of something for which you are truly and deeply grateful. Put yourself back in that beautiful moment. Notice how you feel. Notice the warmth. Notice the sense of peace. Notice the love. Notice the joy. Notice the appreciation. Of course, you can feel fear, anger, worry or frustration before and after you feel grateful, but negative emotions are impossible to feel at the same time as gratitude.

Feeling grateful interrupts whatever negative emotion you're experiencing, long enough to help you shift your perspective and fuel your strength to persevere.

The ability to find and feel true gratitude is the ultimate mind hack – one you can use to triumph over fear. It is a powerful tool that can be learned. On the days when you feel like the walls are caving in, use gratitude as the hook to pull you to safety. In the moments when you are weary and feel like you just can't go on, find something in your life to be grateful for. Something … anything. It's there! Give thanks for the breath you take, the roof over your head, the bed that you sleep in, the blanket that keeps you warm. Give thanks for the senses you have, for the electricity you have, for the running water you have, for the food you eat. Acknowledge your fear but lean into your gratitude.

Now, living in gratitude takes some practise, but the more you practise, the stronger it will be.

CHOOSING AUTHENTICITY AND STEPPING INTO MY POWER

Despite all the fear, all the sickness and all the surgeries, once I received my law degree, I did build a life that I loved – a life I promised myself in that grocery store parking lot!

I moved to Nashville and began my work as a staff attorney for a federal judge; a twenty-one-year career from which I recently retired. It was incredibly meaningful work. As a staff attorney, I was the right hand of the judge. A judge has hundreds of cases at a time, and it's the staff attorney who reads them, looks at every piece of evidence, and analyses and determines how the law applies. The judge got the final say, but I provided the research and the legal advice. In that capacity, I dedicated my life to giving a voice to the voiceless, to seeing people, to hearing people, to making sure every single word they wrote to the court was considered.

And if they met the requirements of the law, they won; if they didn't, they lost. But, regardless of whether they won or lost, I wrote a court decision where they knew that they were seen, they were heard and their voice mattered. The bulk of my work was employment and education discrimination and prison condition cases, but I handled all constitutional claims and civil rights violations. When I began that stage of my career,

WOMEN LIVING FEARLESSLY

I was able to successfully build my life where I could have the impact I wanted and use my voice. But in a way that felt safe, protected.

And then, in January 2019, I found out I had uterine cancer. After nineteen years of fighting for my life, surviving surgery after surgery after surgery, and being a medical miracle, I heard the words that no-one wants to hear: 'Ellie, we have your pathology reports, and I'm sorry, but it's cancer.' Time stopped.

It was time for my fourth major moment of fearlessness. What would I do?

In that moment of deafening silence, I said to myself, *I've been playing small*. And I decided, *No more. Now is the time*. You see, I had built this comfortable, impact-driven bubble where I'd been able to work behind the scenes. I'd been content to be the advisor or the anonymous donor. But right then and there, everything changed. I made a promise to myself: *I don't know how much time I have, but I know this: I'm stepping out of the shadows, and I am stepping up my impact to a global scale. I will impact lives every day I have left on this planet.* My life became clear at that moment.

I stopped hiding behind the curtain. I stopped fearing the light. I stepped out front and really stepped into my own voice, into my own purpose and into my own power. And from that moment on, I have truly lived the life I was meant to live.

CHOOSING EVERY MOMENT

'You are one decision away from a completely different life.'
– Mel Robbins

These four moments of fearlessness have shaped my life by guiding me to clarity – to my why, my passions, my mission and my purpose. This clarity acts as both my fuel and my anchor. It gives me the strength to get up and the grit to persist, while allowing me to remain focused and grounded. I know I was made to change the world. It's my mission and purpose to ignite impact, empower transformation and facilitate change on a global scale. Because my why, my mission and my purpose are bigger than me, they allow me to focus on serving others, which allows me to get out of my own way, choose conviction over convenience, and remain resilient, unbreakable and unstoppable.

Your moments of fearlessness are waiting for you. You just have to be open to them. You don't have to be at ground zero or completely reduced to ashes to grasp them. You don't need to wait for drama or catastrophe. Every moment is an opportunity to decide whether you're staying in the status quo and living from a place of fear or whether it's time to boldly step up and create the life, community and world you envision. What will you choose?

Remember, you're always one decision away from the rest of your life. Be bold. Be fearless. Choose you.

Ellie Shefi is an attorney, advisor, leadership consultant, corporate trainer, keynote speaker, strategist and number-one international bestselling and award-winning author who helps organisations optimise their culture and individuals expand their influence.

As the founder of MTC Consulting, Ellie leverages her more than thirty years of experience in law, business, education and advocacy to help organisations build resilient teams and world-class cultures while developing influential leaders. Serving as a strategic advisor to governments, universities, corporations, entrepreneurs and NGOs, she has successfully helped organisations mitigate their risk, optimise their operations and align their teams.

Dedicated to empowering others to use their voice, Ellie founded Made to Change the World Publishing, a full-service independent publishing house, where she guides aspiring bestselling authors through the writing and publishing process and helps leaders amplify their message so they can scale their impact. In honour of her leadership in the field, Ellie was named Women Changing the World's 2024 Woman in Literature.

A sought-after keynote speaker, Ellie is regularly interviewed in top publications and on podcasts and media channels like Forbes, Entrepreneur, NBC, ABC and CBS, among others, and she hosts the *Free by Design* television show, the *Creating an Impervious Mind* YouTube series and the *You Are Not Your Scars* podcast. At the 2024 Women Changing the World Awards, she received the Woman in Media award, acknowledging her outstanding contributions.

ELLIE D SHEFI

Ellie is also the founder of the Made 2 Change the World Foundation, an emerging nonprofit organisation that equips and empowers the next generation with the tools, resources and strategies they need to create the lives, communities and world they envision.

Website: ellieshefi.com

DEAR YOUNGER ME

Farah Mak

These three words hold immense power – life-changing, transformative and healing.

Allow me to take you on a journey back in time. A journey of reflection, renewal and rejuvenescence. To reach this reawakening, you must venture through the valleys of the unknown, climb arduous mountains and navigate the darkness in search of the light.

The journey won't be easy, but I promise, it will be worth it. Be fully present with me. Open your heart, imagination and intuition to guide you. Embrace each moment with hope, faith, trust and belief.

Are you ready?

Dear Younger Me.

The three words that changed my life, and now, they are about to change yours.

THE LETTER

It was a cold winter's morning. The sun barely crept above the horizon, and the clouds hung heavy and grey. I sat at my desk in my 'creative space', gazing out the window. The clouds, drifting slowly, formed shapes that danced across my window frame.

I had been working closely with a film and television director, a cherished friend and a woman I valued and respected beyond measure. She had become my creative mentor, guiding me in adapting a poem I had written into a screenplay.

For many years, I had poured my heart and soul into this project. Borne from that poem, titled *She Shines,* this work emerged from my own harrowing journey of escaping an abusive relationship, serving as a beacon of hope for women to reclaim their self-worth and transcend the trauma of domestic violence.

The vision was clear, and my purpose was calling me, but the trauma and pain of my past held me back, blocking me from breaking free from the shackles of shame, pain and fear. The heavy clouds outside symbolised the weight on my heart, their dull greyness reflecting the block that held me back. Yet, as they danced across my window frame, they began to take shape, and in that moment, the sun rose through the clouds. It was a symbol of light pushing through the darkness, igniting my inner flame and breaking down the walls of despair.

My mentor had given me a task; to write a letter to my younger self. And so it began: *Dear Younger Me ...*

The words flowed freely, almost uncontrollably, and so did my tears. As my hand scribed, it was as if I was watching a movie of my own life play back, taking me back in time to meet my younger self.

And there she was – lost and afraid.

Writing the letter brought me face-to-face with my inner child, introduced me to my broken self and started the process of healing and renewal. This letter became the birth of my fearlessness.

There is abundant power in writing. There is healing in writing. There is rebirth in writing.

I encourage you to write these three words before you embark on the next part of the journey with me: *Dear Younger Me.*

Leave the words there for now, come back to the process with me, and we will return to your letter soon.

THE PROCESS

From writing those three words, the process of reawakening began. My journey to worthiness took flight, propelling me higher, as I reconnected with my younger self. Yet, this path was also fraught with pain. It demanded courage, kindness and compassion towards myself; to push past the pain points, to forgive both myself and others, and to dismantle the walls I had built to shield myself from the world … and from myself.

As I penned *Dear Younger Me,* I felt a profound shift within. Each word was a step closer to healing, a testament to my resilience. The memories I had long buried resurfaced, and with them came the raw emotions I had avoided for so long. Confronting these emotions was like navigating a labyrinth of shadows, each turn revealing a fragment of my past that needed to be acknowledged and embraced.

The journey was not a linear path but a winding road with peaks of revelation and valleys of doubt. There were moments when the weight of my past seemed insurmountable, but with each breakthrough, I felt a piece of my spirit restored. The pain, once my adversary, became a catalyst for growth, teaching me to be gentle with myself, to honour my journey and to recognise the strength that had always been within me.

Through this process, I learned that healing is not a destination, but an ongoing journey of self-discovery and acceptance. Writing to my younger self was more than an act of reflection, it was an act of reclaiming my power, rediscovering my innate worth, rewriting my narrative and paving the way for a future unbound by past traumas.

As you embark on your own journey, remember that each step forward, no matter how small, is a victory. Embrace the pain, for it is a sign of your courage to heal. And always be kind to yourself – you are worth every ounce of effort it takes to become whole again.

Take a moment to turn back to the words you have scribed … *Dear Younger Me.* Close your eyes and think back to your younger self. Breathe and allow yourself to be fully present with her. How is she feeling? Add to your letter … *I know you're feeling …*

Now come back to the journey with me and trust the process. This is where your transformation begins. The words you write to your younger self are not just words, they are bridges to healing, pathways to understanding and keys to unlocking the potential that lies within. Together, we will navigate this journey.

THE DARK NIGHT OF THE SOUL

We won't linger here long, but we will face it, feel it and acknowledge its presence. For it is often within the dark night of the soul that we discover the key to our own rejuvenation.

Imagine a period of deep isolation and emptiness, where you feel severed from yourself, others and any sense of higher purpose. It seems like a curse, but it is, in fact, a profound transformation.

This darkness serves two vital purposes: awakening the soul and dissolving the ego. As we navigate through it, our soul stirs, urging us toward a higher version of ourselves. Meanwhile, our ego – the identity we've clung to – must be confronted and released. It's a painful shedding of an old skin, making way for a more authentic self to emerge, much like a butterfly strengthening its wings as it breaks free from its chrysalis.

In this space, we are suspended between who we were and who we are becoming. It's a necessary pause, a moment to shed old beliefs and embrace a new reality. Through this process, we transform, revealing the true essence of our soul and stepping into a higher version of ourselves.

The dark night of the soul may visit us once, or it might come many times over a lifetime.

I've experienced many such moments, including recurring triggers, as I began to recall and share in my letter to my younger self. Recently, I had a particularly profound awakening through a dream. It was then that my magical muse, Mavis, first appeared. I woke in a panic, feeling as if I had died. Sitting up in the darkness, I felt like a spirit gazing at my own room.

My husband calmed me, grounding me back to the present, and that's when I remembered the dream and all that my muse had shown me. It was the awakening of my inner writer. The creative floodgates opened wide.

Turn your attention back to your *Dear Younger Me* letter. Acknowledge how she was feeling. Write freely, from your heart to her. Offer her comfort, hope and reassurance. Let her know she is safe and that her future is filled with abundant blessings.

Now, join me as we embark on the journey of healing and rejuvenation. Just like a caterpillar transforming into its authentic, most beautiful form, you have broken through the darkness and your wings have been strengthened. You are ready to heal. Let the rejuvenation begin.

THE HEALING AND REJUVENESCENCE

As I penned that treasured letter to my younger self, opening my heart and soul to reveal the most vulnerable parts of my journey, an overwhelming sense of gratefulness washed over me. I could feel the broken fragments of my past slowly stirring and knitting themselves back together. Each word on the page seemed to mend a piece of my soul, transforming brokenness into newness.

Reflecting on my journey, I saw a tapestry of resilience woven through years of endurance. It became clear that the strength I needed had always been within me. I had always possessed the courage, and I had always carried a hidden sparkle. My younger self, blinded by doubt and insecurity, couldn't see her own brilliance. But now, through the act of writing, I glimpsed my true self and found the love, kindness, respect and admiration she deserved.

The healing brought hope, allowing me to honour my younger self and thank my present self. It rekindled a belief in my future, imbuing the old, broken parts of me with renewed vitality. Writing that letter was more than an act of reflection, it was a process of transformation.

In the depths of that vulnerable moment, I discovered the power of self-love and acceptance. My younger self's struggles had shaped me, and my present self's wisdom could guide her. Through the healing process, I realised I had the power to rejuvenate my spirit, breathing new life into the parts of me that once felt shattered.

The art of writing that letter to my younger self was an act of courage and self-compassion. It brought rejuvenation, not just by mending the past, but by empowering me to embrace the future with new-found strength. The process of transformation was like a gentle breeze, sweeping away the old and making space for the new.

In this journey of healing, I learned that every broken part could be a stepping stone to something beautiful.

Now, let's go faithfully forward together to become the fearless woman you were always meant to be.

THE FEARLESS WOMAN

The powerful lyrics of Andra Day's song resonate in my soul.

In the words of 'Rise Up', I find the strength to rise – not just for myself, but for you and for every woman. Today, I embrace the fearless woman I was created to be. Together, like a lioness pride emerging from the shadows, we shall rise united.

We have journeyed through the dark nights of our souls and emerged into the light of healing and rejuvenation. Our destination is clear; to step into our fearlessness with unwavering courage. We embrace every facet of our beings, love ourselves wholly and forge faithfully ahead on our purpose-driven paths.

Worthy women, this is our call to action. Embrace your journey of healing and self-discovery. Reflect on your past, cherish your present and boldly step into your future. Complete your own *Dear Younger Me* letter and witness the magic of transformation.

Together, let's empower each other, uplift our spirits and shine brighter than ever before. Join us on this journey to fearlessness. Make every moment count and inspire others with your story. You are stronger, braver and more resilient than you realise. Embrace your power and let's change the world – one fearless step at a time!

Farah Mak is an award-winning thought leader, actor, presenter, speaker, writer, facilitator and passionate activist dedicated to ending family violence. Her multifaceted career and unwavering commitment to social change have made her a beacon of hope and a symbol of self-worth.

Recently, Farah returned from London, where she served as the official emcee for the Women Changing the World Awards, co-hosting alongside Sarah Ferguson, Duchess of York, and Dr Tererai Trent. Her impactful work has earned her global recognition, including a silver award for Thought Leader of the Year and a bronze for Social Enterprise, People's Choice. She was also honoured with silver for Most Influential Person of the Year in Australia at the Beam Awards, further establishing her as a symbol of self-worth.

In 2020, Farah launched The Self-Worth Movement, a social enterprise devoted to educating, inspiring and empowering individuals to embrace their self-worth. Through workshops, keynote speaking and soul-affirming products, The Self-Worth Movement seeks to create lasting positive change by boosting confidence, enhancing communication skills and fostering a culture of self-worth in individuals, teams and organisations.

Farah's expertise spans working with individuals, non-profit entities and leadership teams across Australia. She has a proven track record of helping clients achieve their personal and organisational goals by harnessing the power of self-worth. Her holistic approach focuses on developing both individual potential and collective growth.

FARAH MAK

Known for her engaging and energetic presenting style, Farah connects deeply with her audiences, fostering empathy and understanding. Her strength in advocating for social issues brings light to topics often shrouded in darkness. Farah's presentations are not just informative but transformative, leaving a lasting impact.

Farah is also a fearless storyteller, delving into the heart of every story she tells. She creates a safe space for her audience to engage with crucial matters, tackling difficult conversations with hope and the aim of bringing about healing, social justice and meaningful change.

As a popular speaker, presenter and emcee, Farah blends professionalism with warmth, creativity with savvy, and always adds a touch of sparkle. A survivor and thriver, a mother of four and a firm believer in the power of 'glitter' to inspire inner strength, Farah's personal journey from adversity to empowerment serves as a powerful testament to her resilience and dedication.

In addition to her activism and public speaking, Farah portrays Katrina Marshall on the beloved Australian TV series *Neighbours*. She is also set to launch her first children's picture book, *I am Worthy*, from her new series *Sparkle Squad Girls!* This series aims to inspire young girls to recognise their innate worth and discover their core values.

Farah Mak's journey embodies the power of self-worth, resilience and unwavering dedication to social change. Through The Self-Worth Movement and her various endeavours, she continues to inspire and uplift, making a profound impact on the lives of many and solidifying her role as a true symbol of self-worth.

THE BOLD
AND BEAUTIFUL

Florence Kayungwa

'Beauty is not about physical appearance it's about being bold and fearless.'

I was tired of hiding behind the mask and pretending to be someone I wasn't. I was tired of being ordinary, just writing my views and opinions in my small diary every day and never sharing them with anyone or showing up where I was supposed to show up.

As I stood in front of the mirror, I saw a stranger staring back at me. She was timid, afraid to show up and hesitant to speak her mind, sometimes I could ask, *Who are you? I don't know or understand you.* The more I did it, the more I couldn't find a satisfactory answer. As a young woman in her early twenties, I know I have a choice to make. I could continue living a life that wasn't mine, deep inside, knowing if I continued on that pathway, it was going to silence me forever. Or I could take a leap of faith and become that girl who is bold and beautiful. I decided to face my fears and go for what I want; making sure I advocate for girls' education, even though it's not a common goal in my community.

I began to shed the skin of conformity, embracing my quirks and flaws. I challenged the status quo one day by saying **'LET GIRLS LEARN'** and let us break down the barriers, once and for all. The responses I received from people around me encouraged me to see the world in a different light; to see the beauty in the imperfect and the strength in vulnerability. This made me realise that it's now the time to go for what I want and be the voice of the voiceless, because there will be someone counting on me to stand up and be their advocate.

Growing up in a marginalised community, I saw firsthand and

experienced the devastating impact of the shortage of resources. I missed school and watched as friends dropped out, succumbing to poverty, teenage pregnancy and hopelessness. My mission is to change the narrative, but it's not easy, it needs someone who is fearless. I took the bold step of speaking up because I want to live a good life. For life to be positive, it should be connected to the greater good that is making the world a better place for others.

Sometimes I face resistance, but I always persist. I face intimidation, ridicule and, at times, even threats, but my inner strength, resilience and compassion always shine brighter like a little torch in the dark. As I am growing, so is my influence. I share my vision with world leaders and educators. My message is clear: **'LET GIRLS LEARN'** because educated girls are more likely to make informed decisions and it's in line with the United Nations Sustainable Development Goal number four, which focuses on ensuring inclusive and equitable quality education and promoting lifelong learning opportunities for all. Every child deserves access to quality education regardless of their zip code or socioeconomic status.

There is a famous saying:

Show me your friends and I will tell you more about you. – Unknown

I make sure to surround myself with women who inspire me; those who embody the same bold and beautiful spirit. Together, we lift each other up, celebrating our differences and supporting our dreams.

I am bold and beautiful and I am proud to be me. I am a work of art in progress, a masterpiece of imperfection and strength. I am unstoppable.

'THAT'S NOT WHAT OTHER WOMEN DO.'

My motivation comes from listening, reading and hearing some of the giants who have come before me; Malala Yousafzai, a Pakistani activist for girls' education, Florence Nightingale, the pioneer of the modern

WOMEN LIVING FEARLESSLY

nursing and founder of the Red Cross, and Angelina Jolie actress and UNHCR Goodwill ambassador, supporting refugees and displaced people worldwide. In my mind, I told myself this was evidence that the women empowerment project had already been started and achieved. These women defined the right to question a woman's character and her urge to dream big and create a better world for others. Women had come so far. I learned we no longer needed to worry about objectification or misogyny. Instead, it is time for us to join the frat party of trending culture and mark the death of fear and patriarchy. Even if they say, 'That's not what other women do.'

According to my culture, marriage is more important than your dreams as an individual. If we have big dreams, we are constantly reminded, 'That's not what other women do,' so in every family, when it comes to a girl child, they prioritise marriage above all else. When a girl reaches sixteen years old, there is the constant question, 'When are you going to get married?'

Yes, having a family is a good thing, but there is more to life, and we must focus on achieving our dreams that are tied to a greater good. The kind of pressure forced on many girls to rush into marriage, without a single penny to their names, creates a dependence syndrome and also kills many dreams.

One of my community members asked me why I chose to be an education advocate and when am I going to quit, because, 'That's not what other good women do. It's only acceptable if a man is doing it.' My response was, 'Can man and woman not work together to find solutions that work so we can all change the world together?' In the African context we say, '*Musha mukadzi*' (*a woman is the strength of the house*). *So I am a responsible woman who is working hard to make a fortune for my family and changing the world for others*. I did that until they started to call me the dream girl.

I salute every woman who chooses to have a career and follow her dreams, rather than waiting for things to happen.

Some women that inspire me for being bold and beautiful, and living fearlessly, are Christie Hefner and Linda Harvard. They were the chair and CFO of The Playboy Group until 2009; brave women working in an industry that many other women might judge them for. However, they are progressive thinkers who advocate for women in a variety of ways.

Tererai Trent International is also an organisation of female executives and business owners who provide mentoring programs and scholarships, providing universal education for boys and girls, and focusing on gender parity. These women are inspiring examples of women living fearlessly; they are bold and also beautiful. This is a fuel to my dream and the pathway I have chosen.

'GOOD GIRLS DON'T HUSTLE.'

I am not surprised to say that social media, as well as huge number of printed book media, is filled with hundreds of male CEOs and self-made entrepreneurs who tout the power of wealth and the justification for achieving it. But if you are a woman, in my culture it seems, it's frowned upon by both men and women. It's impolite … it's not something good girls do.

Good girls don't talk about money or businesses, running an enterprise or even a non-profit organisation. Certainly, they don't claim it as a life goal, regardless of their reason why. **What I have learnt is, 'You get what you get, and you don't throw a fit.'**

That meant I should be happy with whatever life handed me, gracious and thankful for whatever came my way. But deep down I knew, and believe, that everyone is in control of their destiny. You can own something big, talk about money, change the world, regardless of your gender. And no-one should force you to settle for less or tell you what good girls do or not do.

There is a big difference between gratitude for your life and blind acceptance of whatever comes your way; as for me I want more. I want more experience, more knowledge and the ability to help others who are in difficult situations, because I know how they feel. I grew up hearing those words ... 'Good girls don't hustle.' My guardians, teachers and even friends whispered them to me as if it was a **truth** I needed to accept. But I never did.

One day, I was stunned when someone asked, 'We see what you're doing, and it's great, but when are you going to quit?' They didn't like the idea of me being an activist. For the first time in my life, I understood that other people don't always agree with the life you imagine for yourself. They didn't like the idea of a young girl standing up, wanting to be heard. Even if you are strong and are committed to your goal, it's hard not to second-guess yourself or take on guilt when it's coming at you from every angle. *'I was like a piece of glass that gets thrown into the ocean, other people's opinion became my waves, their judgements the sand I was tossed against over and over, until it began to chip away at all my jagged edges.'*

I know I am not the only one who has ever bumped up against the expectations of others and then backed down because of them. In a desire to find community, I constantly seek out other women in leadership, and what I find again and again are bold women doing just what I have done. They were told that good girls don't hustle, but they went against the trend.

I am telling you my story in the hopes that, if you are like us, you know there is a tribe of ladies who feel the same way, even if not everyone has found the courage to say it out loud yet. It's okay to want something more for your life.

I love women who challenge the status quo. I love someone who is unabashed about what they want for their lives and refuses to let anyone talk them out of it. From my experience, society tends to raise boys to go after what they want and tends to raise girls to go after boys. I am here to tell you that it doesn't matter what society thinks about your dreams. All that really matters is how badly you want those dreams and what you are willing to do to make them happen.

Are you a hard worker and a dreamer? Me too. Do you secretly want to be, but are afraid of what other people might think or say? I have been there. For many women, the weight of other people's opinion will be too big a burden to carry. They won't be able to step outside the safety net because they are scared. But that's not us. We are willing to go after it, we are willing to be audacious and we are willing to take a risk because the chance to live into our full potential is worthy of any backlash that comes our way. Some say, 'Good girls don't hustle,' but when someone tells me that, I just smile and say, 'Watch me.'

'IT'S ALL BEEN DONE BEFORE.'

It's one of those things we all do, right? We stop ourselves from writing that book, opening that business, building that app, starting that non-profit, because someone else has already done it.

Well, of course, they have! But, sister, everything that sounds interesting or cool or seems like something you might want to try already exists, it's already been done! But why is it that we don't let that deter us in any other scenario, unless we are pursuing something BIG?

It's because we need an excuse.

The fact that someone has already done the thing you are dreaming of should not be a deterrent, it should be a sign that you are onto something good. You stop yourself from trying because you think it's already been done, but it hasn't yet been done by you.

You talk yourself out of something you haven't even attempted, because you think you can't measure up to someone else's version of what you want. But this particular excuse is not about your skill; this excuse is about your fear.

If you find yourself worried about the idea that someone else has done it before you, you need to flip the script on whether that's a bad thing. If someone else has done it, you can research and model their behaviour, and test out your own theories, while using their road map as some kind of guidance. You can combine their *how* with your *why* to create something epic.

I was born 27 September 2001, I am a keynote speaker, published author, menstrual health advocate and a fundraiser who is fighting period poverty in rural areas of Zimbabwe where two in every five girls miss five days a month of school due to period poverty.

Global award-winner non-profit award (bronze) courtesy of Women Changing the World. The awards were presented by the Dutchess of York Sarah Ferguson and Zimbabwe-renowned humanitarian and Oprah Winfrey's all-time favourite guest Dr Tererai Trent. I also won Philanthropist of the Year 2024 Zimbabwe courtesy of Mega Fest Holdings. I am a news reporter at NRTV and a media and communications director at Leaders of All Nations International.

EDUCATION
BA Honors Film Radio and Television Production.
Certificate of completion course on sustainable civil society organisation.
Certificate of completion sign language and special needs.

SHATTERING GLASS CEILINGS

Iris Mhlanga

I was stunned and speechless. Having just checked my emails, I discovered that I'd been nominated for another international award. This would be my thirty-second award nomination in the last couple of months. And I still don't know what created such a flurry of international recognition, but importantly, it's led to global interest and awareness in the work I do, enabling me to support more and more people.

I honestly can't believe how much my life has changed since a simple act of kindness catapulted my life onto a completely unexpected path. A woman's personal growth can be likened to a phoenix rising from the ashes. If you'd met me five years ago, you'd unlikely recognise the person I am today, accepting awards and honorary degrees, public speaking and running an organisation that supports over five thousand people and feeds 1,200 orphans every day.

Yes ... now, I am *a woman living fearlessly*. But it wasn't always that way ...

For many years, I've now realised I lived my life as a victim – in the grip of emotional and financial abuse. With two young children, one with a physical disability needing extra care, for a long time, I didn't see what was happening right in front of me. To be honest, I had no idea at the time just how trapped I was. I was in a marriage where my husband did everything for me, but gave me little emotional support or respect, slowly eating away at my self-worth. At that time in my life, I would never have been able to do what I do now. I wouldn't have believed I could do it, as I hadn't really done *anything* for myself since I first met him. I'm sure my ex-husband is looking on now, amazed, and watching in surprise, as I share on social media the work we are doing to support the vulnerable and needy in Zimbabwe and beyond, to give them hope and support them to find ways to improve their situation and make something of their lives.

I understand what it means to have someone believe in you when you're in a vulnerable situation and to have hope that tomorrow will be 'better'. I too have been significantly vulnerable, both financially and emotionally. At one time, my children and I were extremely lucky not to be left homeless, after my ex-husband announced, without my prior knowledge, that he'd sold everything we had. We had to start from the ground up, and when you're at rock bottom, the only way is up. From the depths of adversity and despair, there lies the potential for profound transformation, because everything must change, but it takes courage and strength of spirit.

***

Growing up, it was just me and Mum living in a small flat that she owned. I've always had the wonderful support of my mother's family, my grandparents being an amazing influence in my life, but growing up without brothers and sisters, while Mum worked hard every day to support us, I was given quite a bit of responsibility as a young child. As far back as I was able, I worked during school holidays and after school, with jobs Mum found for me. She set up a joint bank account, that I was required to contribute to, and taught me how to pay bills and buy groceries. She definitely taught me a lot about money management, but looking back, I guess it was a lot of responsibility for a young child.

I think Mum knew she was sick a long time before she let anyone else know about it. She didn't want to worry my grandparents, but in my last year of high school, she was so sick that she had to go and live with them so they could care for her. I stayed alone in the flat during the week and visited them on weekends. I had to be close to school and my after-school jobs during the week. It was an important year; I needed to achieve my best possible results in my exams and continue to save my money, as my intention was to travel to London and study medicine. My cousin lived there, and it was all I thought about … until Mum got sick.

I didn't like living alone in the flat. It was a difficult time in my life, but through the adversity, I managed to get the results I needed and my plan to move to London was very much on track. When Mum was well enough to return home, she had changed. She withdrew any intimacy, avoiding me, sometimes even avoiding *looking* at me. I can only look back on that time and imagine she knew that she didn't have much time left, and thought she was helping me by not keeping me close, but it certainly was a confusing time for me as a teenager.

I'd been working after school at a car sales yard, and it was there that I met my (soon-to-be) husband. I had already worked with him for about a year before we started dating. I don't remember thinking anything romantic about him during that time, my thoughts were too preoccupied with other important things. When he asked me to go out on a date, I was a little shocked and told him I needed to check with my parents first, to which he replied, 'Oh, you don't need to worry about that.' Of course, I was confused by that remark, but it turned out that he had already asked my grandfather and mum if he could date me, and they'd agreed it was okay. When I got home that evening, my mum brought it up before I even plucked up the courage to talk to her about it! 'You'll need to buy some new shoes and a nice dress for your date on the weekend,' she said, without any prompting from me.

I certainly wasn't expecting a long-term relationship, and I hadn't told him about my plans to move to London, but he always seemed to know things about me that I hadn't told him. He and Mum had a close and friendly relationship, which intrigued me, and very soon after we started dating, she suggested that he stay with us in the flat, as he lived out on a farm 40km away from work and his commute would take him a couple of hours every day. It was a good option for him, and so, very suddenly, we were living together.

Sometimes, events can happen very quickly and unexpectedly.

I guess I did feel rather powerless in that situation, it was almost like Mum 'handed me over' to him. I was still only seventeen at the time. It was from that point that he took over *everything*. Both our families approved of the relationship, and suddenly I felt part of another family; I was treated like the daughter-in-law. He paid all my bills and brought me flowers every day, taking care of my every need. It happened so fast, and I was happy as he did give me lots of attention, and now, all my money could go into savings for my trip to London.

One day, just after he'd dropped me at work, he returned, acting odd, and insisted, 'You have to take the day off.' He was always doing things out of the blue like that, taking me to beautiful places on the spur of the moment, and he never left me with an option to say no. But that day was different. I went to the boss asking if I could take the day off. To my surprise he said, 'Take the week off.' I realised he must have already spoken to my boss, but I still didn't know what was happening. He took me to my grandparents, and seeing them crying, I realised my mum had passed away. They told me I would need to lock up the flat and live with them; my boyfriend and I couldn't continue living under the same roof without an adult (without being married) due to our strict African traditions.

He was very supportive during that time, he arranged everything – he had a gift for doing things around me, so I didn't have to do anything. He had brought all my clothes with him, so I didn't have to go back to the flat. He locked up the flat and took care of things while my world was spinning. The crazy thing was that the day after Mum passed away was the day I had scheduled with a travel agent to book my flight to the UK. Obviously, my family said I couldn't go.

In her will, Mum left a note to say she thought my new boyfriend would be able to look after me. We had only been together for a few months. During the whirlwind of emotions, it wasn't long before we had arranged a traditional wedding; his family even paid a dowry. We moved back into the flat together, but very quickly the cracks began to show. Living together as husband and wife, I thought I could do nothing about it … I truly believed that I belonged to him. I felt he was the 'boss of me'.

After a few years together, we had our son, but the cracks were getting bigger. I started hearing stories from neighbours about 'other women', but I would never believe their gossip; I didn't believe he would do something like that. He had also started a business, but I wasn't a part of it and had very little knowledge of what he did on a daily basis. By the time our daughter came along, we had moved out of the flat into a big four-bedroom house, and he took care of everything. At that time, he literally did everything for me. I didn't even go to buy groceries or pay bills. Of course, I was taking care of my children, but I was bored.

Something told me I needed to get back to my original plan; to get higher qualifications that could help me. Though he tried to convince me otherwise. 'You don't need to go back to study. You're the wife of a prominent person now, you don't need to do anything.' But I knew I did.

I came up with an arrangement with my cousin where I paid their share to look after our grandparents, and they enrolled me and paid for my online studies. It meant my husband didn't know what I was doing the whole time I was studying. When I achieved my degree, he was actually angry about it! I was confused; of course, surely, he should be happy at my achievement. Instead, he was angry that I'd done something for myself without his knowledge. I realised I had no idea what he was doing on a day-to-day basis either.

It came to a point in 2018, when we had to move out of our big house, because the rent hadn't been paid. I was lucky to be able to secure a flat for us to have a roof over our heads, something I had to do. I was shocked, but not unhappy, that he didn't move in with us. What a transition. Suddenly I had to put on my 'big girl' pants and do everything for myself. I had to dig deep and remember a time when I used to pay bills and work for my own money.

It seems our marriage ended as quickly and suddenly as it began.

Every painful experience has had a hand in building my resilience, and I can no longer recognise the woman I used to be. Looking at my reflection in the mirror, there now stands a distinguished philanthropist and author. This too has happened quickly. A moment in time when I chose to live fearlessly, helping a homeless man, as a crowd gathered around to watch rather than 'help', spurred me on to use my voice on social media. Finding my voice in that moment has led, so unexpectedly, to meeting amazing people and growing a charitable organisation that now has international recognition and helps thousands of people every day.

Now I have no choice but to live fearlessly. Embracing fear has enabled me to welcome a brighter future for myself, my children and anyone I can inspire to break free from fear and choose life. I don't know what will happen in the future, but if the past is anything to go by, and if I trust and live fearlessly, things will happen quickly, just as they are meant to.

I no longer know where or what my ex-husband is doing these days, but a mutual friend contacted me recently, and the words my ex used to describe me to him were clear:

SHE HAS FOUND HER VOICE!

IRIS MHLANGA

Iris Zemza Nozizwe Mhlanga is a philanthropist and pharmacologist; she has dedicated her life to making a difference in the lives of the underprivileged, marginalised and vulnerable communities in Zimbabwe. Her unwavering commitment to humanitarian efforts has transformed countless lives and earned her over thirty international nominations for prestigious awards, including the 2024 Women Changing the World Global Awards and the Women Icon 2024 Awards.

Iris' journey began in a family of helpers. Her father, a founding member and former president of Highlanders Football Club in Zimbabwe, always looked after vulnerable communities, especially orphans. He named Iris 'Nozizwe' which translates to 'mother of nations'. This upbringing instilled in her a heart for caring for the less fortunate. After her father's passing, Iris continued his legacy by assisting a destitute disabled man. Word spread, and others sought her help. Through social media, she shared her story, and the community rallied to support her cause. Today, the Nozizwe Mother of Nations Trust feeds 1,200 orphans daily and pays school fees for a thousand more, benefiting over five thousand people across Zimbabwe.

A JOURNEY OF STRENGTH AND KINDNESS

MY PATH TO RELATIONSHIP-CENTRED LEADERSHIP AND BACK TO ME

Justine Cox

Imagine a world where leading with strength and kindness is every organisation's superpower. This is my purpose, but it's not one I discovered overnight. It's a journey I've grown into – a path that has led me not only to empower others but back to myself.

I'm writing from the lush jungles of Ubud, Bali, where the scent of incense lingers in the air, and the soft rustle of leaves reminds me of the quiet power within us all. As I take a deep breath, grateful to be living one of my dreams, I reflect on how far I have come.

As a relationship-centred leader, I aim to connect, build trust and inspire you to challenge yourself, so you can grow into the leader you're meant to be. I hope my story ignites a fire in you and helps you discover the strength to take action. I also hope it encourages you to find the kindness to embrace all of you, so you can step into your best self.

You, too, hold the power to lead with purpose and courage. Together, we can leave the world better than we found it, but that only happens when we are at our best, more often.

BLUE-COLLAR BEGINNINGS

Growing up in a blue-collar family in a small coastal town, I witnessed firsthand the relentless effort my parents put into providing for us. They juggled five jobs, ensuring we had enough. My childhood was filled with lessons on the value of hard work, resilience and the power of community. We were a sporting family, which taught me the importance of being a team player and striving for excellence. My dad's words, 'If you sign up to be part of a team, they deserve your best every time,' became my mantra and shaped my leadership style. Mum's approach to life was to support from the sidelines, be understanding of others, to show her love through acts of kindness and never say a bad word about anyone.

EMBRACING LEADERSHIP

I didn't set out to be a leader, but life had other plans. Leadership roles seemed to find me; from vice-captain in primary and high school to captain of my under-tens netball team. It taught me that respect is earned through attitude and actions, not titles. I was fifteen and captain of our representative netball team when I was presented with my first real leadership challenge. The team was unhappy with a teammate's lack of effort and commitment, and I had to address it. It was a delicate balance of strength and kindness, and it taught me a vital lesson; true leadership requires courage, firmness and empathy. I also realised that the reality of challenging conversations was, often, not as tough as the anxiety-inducing stories we build up in our heads.

FINDING MY PROFESSIONAL PATH

My professional journey began with a brief stint as a secretary (an act of defiance against my parents), but I was fired eleven months later. I transitioned into hospitality, drawn by my love for people, which led me to a human resources career. After struggling to break into an HR generalist role and fuelled by a thirst for travel, I backpacked for two years and landed a role in *The Guardian* newspaper's HR team in London.

Back home in Australia, at twenty-eight, I secured my first state HR management role. It was a male-dominated environment; I was the only female, and the youngest, in the leadership team. It was tough, there were corporate politics, big personalities and personal agendas. I never really felt like an equal. However, my state manager's support, characterised by accountability and compassion, helped me navigate this challenging terrain. I learnt resilience and the value of building genuine relationships and connecting with the person behind the resume.

WOMEN LIVING FEARLESSLY

HOLDING ON THROUGH HEARTACHE

My world was rocked when my mum was diagnosed with cancer at fifty. I was thirty. As I watched her on life support, I felt a profound emptiness. She was my lighthouse. Her resilience and determination during her courageous three-year battle equally inspired and saddened me. The benefit of knowing that death is coming is that you get the opportunity to have conversations you previously didn't dare have. I took that opportunity, which helped me see life through my mum's eyes. The experience was raw, intense, and at times, incredibly hard. It was also warm, soft and beautiful – a crucial lesson in getting out of my own way, seeing life from others' perspectives and understanding the value of open, candid and trusting conversations.

I held my mum's hand when she took her last breath and didn't let go for three hours. In the days leading up to her funeral, I sat beside her every day. I could not imagine a life without her. Being with her comforted me. Her funeral was the worst day of my life. I didn't want to say goodbye; it took three attempts before I let the driver actually drive me there and I still don't know how I got through the eulogy. I felt a consuming and relentless ache as an inescapable void settled in me. I was angry for her; who's kidding, I was angry for me. For the memories and conversations we would never have. For the love and support I was losing. That she was leaving me when I still needed her. I had no idea how I would live again. So, I existed.

I shrank my life, stepped into the shadows and hoped no-one noticed me. I didn't have the strength to get out of a marriage I didn't really want and went to a dark place. I felt alone and disconnected from the world. The doctor prescribed medication, but I was too scared to take it, fearing I might never come back. My escape was work; there, I could bury myself, put on my corporate suit of armour and immerse myself in the grind. It was a relief because at home the heartache returned. Weekends of retreating into myself, drinking too much alcohol to numb the pain and talking too little to avoid the reality that I had to live without my beautiful mum. While my personal life shrunk, my professional life flourished.

Through my leadership I felt strong, holding space for others that I could not hold for myself. I was living two separate lives. Leaning into my leadership role enabled me to hold on.

FROM BREAKING POINT TO BREAK THROUGH

In HR you often get, 'Yes, but here at the coal face that won't work,' so I decided to test my HR theories. I took on a state operations role for a national not-for-profit, in a sector I knew nothing about, and focused on what I knew: people and relationships. I was quickly promoted to general manager, leading a twenty-four-seven high-risk, sensitive service (two states and a territory, overseeing 450 people and an $80 million budget). I was then asked to take on the national HR team as well.

This was the first time I experienced the *power of purpose.* When things got tough, I noticed my people would hold onto the difference we were making. It became increasingly clear that having a strong sense of purpose provided clarity and direction and served as a source of motivation and resilience.

But it didn't take long to realise traditional leadership programs didn't equip me with the right tools for success. The stress and overwhelm nearly led to burnout. I reached a breaking point and thought, *I can't do this!* This coincided with my marriage finally crumbling.

Following a particularly aggressive and hurtful argument with my husband, I curled into the foetal position on the floor and rocked back and forth, crying. The only thing I could think of was, *How do I end my life? I can't do this anymore.* I hit my lowest point. I was failing at home and at work.

I felt alone, embarrassed, anxious and scared. When I looked in the mirror, I didn't recognise the woman looking back at me. I had lost myself, and it was from that suffocating, dark place that I decided I needed to find myself again.

I retreated to Bali for rest and reflection and realised, that for the first time in my life, I had no goals. So that's where I started. By focusing on what was possible and moving towards it, I could ensure my experiences would shape me, not break me.

I tackled work first. I needed to feel like I was winning again and developed a system that enabled me to lead and grow a significant part of an organisation, outside my primary expertise. This system, now called my 3P relationship-centred leadership system, helped me reclaim eight hours of time per week, feel more confident, less overwhelmed and achieve better results.

Next was my marriage. I had to be honest with myself and with my husband. I did not want to be married.

He didn't let go easily, but I persisted, drawing on my strength and tried to maintain kindness (slipping often but never giving up). Despite swearing never to return to my hometown after Mum's death, deep down, I knew it was where I belonged. So, I left and went back. Now, when I walk into my home, where I held Mum's hand as she took her last breath, it feels like a warm hug and brings a smile to my face.

Moving home was about reconnecting with my support network and with me, so I could grow into the person I could be. I journalled, meditated, exercised, saw a therapist, spent time alone and leaned on my people. This period of reflection enabled me to see that I had, in fact, chosen to give others the power to shape my life. My power. So I decided to take it back.

As you read this, you may be thinking, *Was it really that simple? My life, problems and challenges are hard, complex, insurmountable!* I hear similar responses through my coaching, but my experience tells me that *deciding* is the simplest thing you can do.

So here's an experiment for you – remember you can't fail an experiment, they are, by nature, about testing and learning: Think about a challenge you have. What are you stuck on? Hold that in your mind. What have you decided about that challenge that's holding you back? What different choice can you make, or perspective can you adopt, that will move you forward? If it still feels overwhelming choose the smallest step possible. How do you feel? If you need some help, reach out and ask a mentor, coach or trusted colleague. You can think many things about any situation and they can all be valid, look for the optimistic choice.

AN ERA OF ENDURANCE

In my forties, my resilience was tested to its core. I faced the emotional turmoil of a divorce, the profound joys and challenges of motherhood, the loss of my beloved Nan, and the complexities of menopause, each hurdle coming one after the other. Amidst these trials, I embraced new professional roles, including business owner and becoming chair of a community bank board.

I fell in love and, against all odds, fell pregnant naturally. Despite significant challenges, including placenta praevia and an eighty-seven-day hospital stay with the constant threat to my baby's and my own life, I brought home my beautiful, healthy baby boy, Nash. I view the hospital time as a gift that allowed me to slow down and prepare for motherhood, ultimately making me a better mum.

When Nash was six months old, I started thinking about the future and decided to start a business and build the life I dreamed of. I wanted to create a purpose-driven business that grew the next generation of strong and kind leaders, while also experiencing as much of the world as possible. I found the strength to start Leaders Change Room from my commitment to an experimental mindset – testing and learning without fear of failure.

But the traditional family fairytale wasn't to be. While we had been a great couple, living together as a family created tension that wasn't healthy for us. I found myself at another crossroads, facing the hardest decision yet: one that would affect my son and his relationship with his dad and family. Although I still loved my son's father, our relationship had changed, and I felt like I was beginning to lose myself again. Nash was four, and my business was three. Adjusting to life as a solo mom was tough, and stepping out on my own without a safety net took immense courage. Yet, I knew in my heart it was the right choice. During these challenges, one of the most daunting battles I faced was supporting my dad through his diagnosis of chronic traumatic encephalopathy (CTE) and witnessing the devastating impact on his life.

I learned to hold onto hope and lightness, while also allowing myself space to process loss and sadness. This tumultuous decade illuminated valuable lessons; *my purpose provides clarity in times of uncertainty, the quality of my relationships determines my ability to create impact and healthy habits offer structure and stability during chaos.*

LIVING AND LEADING WITH PURPOSE   MY WAY

My journey has shaped the development of my 3P relationship-centred leadership system; the heart of transforming traditional leadership into a more purpose-driven and impactful approach. Anchored in *purpose, people and process*, this system represents my evolution from chaos to calm, from self-doubt to self-awareness, and from traditional to relationship-centred leadership. At the core of my approach are strength, kindness and trust.

Let's create a world where leadership is every organisation's superpower, *and it starts with us*. I have learnt to confidently say *this is who I am, this is the life I want and this is what my legacy will be*. I hope my story helps you to do the same … especially when it feels hard.

So here I am, the smell of incense dancing in the air, Ubud's jungle stretching out before me, experimenting with living and working somewhere new. Bali, with its soothing rhythms and rich culture, has become my sanctuary – a space where my soul feels truly at home. But my writing must come to an end. It's time to pick up my son from his Balinese school where he, too, is experimenting with a new culture and people.

Nash inspires me to live and lead with purpose, building a legacy that leaves the world a better place. My personal and professional challenges helped to shape the woman I am today, living life on my terms, leaning into my strength and kindness. I will continue confronting my self-doubt, challenging my negative narratives, choosing optimism and standing in my power. To show up and be my best more often. For my son, my mum and me. For a better tomorrow.

I invite you to join me on this journey.

Justine Cox is a mum, friend, reciprocity advocate, intrepid traveller, book club member and Audrey Hepburn fan. She is also a relationship-centred leadership specialist and the visionary founder of Leaders Change Room. With over two decades of experience transforming leaders and organisations, she has led teams of all sizes, from small, close-knit groups to large, complex organisations. Justine is known for supporting managers in being their best, driving change and fostering high-performance environments grounded in trust and relationships. Her hands-on experience in hybrid and remote leadership, human resources and operations makes her an invaluable resource for senior leaders and their management teams.

Justine has a proven track record of guiding leaders through leadership challenges. Her programs are grounded in neuroscience, positive psychology, coaching techniques and behaviour change strategies. She has a remarkable talent for simplifying complex concepts and asking insightful questions that inspire transformative shifts in people.

Leaders Change Room offers leadership development programs, micro-learning and coaching for purpose-driven organisations aiming to make leadership their superpower. Programs focus on upskilling managers to become leaders who inspire people, unite teams and achieve consistent results. Her signature group coaching program, Leadership Lift, exemplifies her expertise. It provides managers with a simple system to help them be at their best more often, get the best out of their team and achieve more with the time they have. Leadership Lift is about helping leaders rediscover their confidence and create environments where their people can consistently perform at their best, transitioning managers from hands-on workers to leaders who effectively delegate and empower their teams.

Justine's educational background is extensive and diverse. She holds a bachelor's of business and a master's of management, along with a diploma in neuroscience of leadership and a diploma of positive psychology. Her credentials also include advanced executive coaching certification (IECL), change management practitioner certification (ADKAR by Prosci) and leadership behaviour practitioner certification (LSI Human Synergistics). This knowledge base enables her to help leaders better understand themselves, build trusting relationships and lead without the overwhelm that often comes with people leadership.

Throughout her career, Justine has guided hundreds of leaders in developing self-awareness, building trust within their teams and leading effectively without succumbing to the stress and time pressures that come with managing people. She is particularly dedicated to helping early to mid-career leaders in small- to medium-sized enterprises (SMEs) unlock their potential and create teams people don't want to leave.

Justine lives in a small coastal community on the south-east coast of Australia, where she continues to make a significant impact on leadership teams and managers. In addition to her work with Leaders Change Room, she serves as chair of both the Bendigo Community Bank National Council and the Community Bank South Coast. Her commitment to leadership extends beyond her professional endeavours, applying the same principles of strength and kindness to her community work, building trust and unlocking potential in every aspect of her life.

LIVING FEARLESSLY IS NOT THE ABSENCE OF FEAR, BUT THE COURAGE TO FACE IT

Katy Garner

For a significant part of my life, I haven't been okay. On the outside, it might have seemed like I was holding it all together, but on the inside, I was battling something that felt overwhelming – my mental health. Obsessive-compulsive disorder (OCD), particularly intrusive thoughts and anxiety, have always been a part of my journey. These are things that many of us deal with but rarely talk about. We shy away from sharing our struggles, fearing judgement or misunderstanding. For me, those intrusive thoughts weren't just fleeting – they were paralysing. They made me question my safety, my abilities and my future.

At one point, I didn't believe I could run a business, let alone a national or global one. The idea of being responsible for something that large felt insurmountable. I was consumed by fear. Fear of being seen, fear of failing and fear of leaving my family behind when I travelled. Flying became a particular source of anxiety, as did the irrational fear that something terrible would happen to me while I was away. My mind would race, and intrusive thoughts would spiral out of control, leaving me feeling frozen in fear.

This struggle isn't something that I moved past overnight. It took time, support and the unwavering presence of my loved ones. My doctors, amazing friends, my family and especially my sister, all played a part in helping me slowly but surely move through the storm. And while some days are better than others, I'm proud to say that I now run a global business, one that requires me to fly internationally – a concept that once seemed impossible for me to grasp.

But even as I stand here today, having achieved more than I once thought possible, those feelings haven't entirely disappeared. Anxiety is still part of my life. And recently, I've noticed it creeping back in. The fears, the intrusive thoughts – they still have a way of showing up unannounced. The difference now is that I recognise the signs. I know that when my anxiety starts to escalate, it's my body and mind telling me to slow down. It's a signal to take a step back, to rest, to reconnect with myself and the people I love.

In those moments, I do something I never used to give myself permission to do – I take a break. I take a weekend off. I reach out to friends and spend time with them. I shift my focus back to my wellness, mentally and physically. It's not about running away from my responsibilities or my success, but about ensuring I can sustain both. After all, you can't pour from an empty cup.

I think what surprises people most about this is that, from the outside, it often looks like I have everything together. People see the success, the awards, the businesses, the travel, the big events, and they assume I must have conquered all of my fears. But that's not the full picture. Yes, I am successful, and yes, I am deeply grateful for the life I have built. But that doesn't mean everything is perfect all the time. And I think it's important for us to be honest about that.

It's easy to look at someone else's life and think, *They've got it all figured out*. We see the curated versions of each other's lives on social media, in interviews or in passing conversations, and we make assumptions. We assume people aren't struggling, that they aren't dealing with their own battles. But the truth is, many of us are fighting battles no-one else can see. That's why we have to be kind. We have to ask, 'Are you okay?' not just once, but consistently. We need to check in with each other, not only when it's convenient or when we notice something might be wrong, but because sometimes the hardest battles are the ones fought in silence.

This is a call for empathy, for understanding and for action. It's a reminder that we all need support at different points in our lives. And it's also a message to anyone reading this who might be feeling the weight of their own struggles: it's okay to reach out. It's okay to ask for help. It's okay to admit that things aren't perfect. None of us are perfect, and none of us have to be.

I've learned that the more open I am about my journey, the more I give others permission to do the same. Vulnerability can be terrifying, especially when you're in a position of leadership or success. There's a pressure to keep up appearances, to always be 'on', to show the world that you've got it all under control. But that's not reality. And I've come to realise that real strength lies in embracing our vulnerabilities, not in hiding them.

This is what living fearlessly means to me – not the absence of fear, but the courage to face it. It means allowing myself to be seen, not just in my successes, but in my challenges as well. It means recognising that asking for help is not a sign of weakness, but a demonstration of strength. It means understanding that it's okay to slow down, to take breaks and to prioritise my mental health without feeling guilty for doing so.

For anyone who is struggling right now, I want you to know that you are not alone. There are days when I still feel anxious, when the intrusive thoughts come back, and I question everything. But I've learned to lean on the people around me, to trust that I have built a strong foundation and to know that these moments will pass. I have also learned that it's okay to talk about mental health. In fact, it's essential that we do.

We need to create spaces where these conversations are normalised, where we can talk openly about our fears, our anxieties and our mental health without feeling ashamed. Because when we do that, we not only heal ourselves, but we also give others the opportunity to heal alongside us.

In the end, living fearlessly isn't about never feeling fear. It's about feeling the fear and showing up anyway. It's about giving ourselves grace when things feel overwhelming. It's about knowing that we don't have to have it all figured out all the time. And it's about remembering that we are all in this together, supporting each other through the highs and the lows.

So the next time you look at someone and think they've got it all together, take a moment to ask, 'Are you okay?' You might be surprised by the answer. And in doing so, you might just help them – and yourself – live a little more fearlessly.

Award-winning entrepreneur and author Katy Garner is the co-founder of Women Changing The World Press, The Women's Changing The World Awards and AusMumpreneur.

Katy's purpose is to support, educate and inspire women to create businesses that work for them. With a background in publishing, events and community engagement, she's passionate about being a voice for women and has been active in advocating for more recognition of the work of Australian women in business with local, state and federal politicians, to encourage more funding and support for women in business. Katy has been on the board of the Queensland Small Business Advisory Council.

For the past fifteen years Katy has organised the AusMumpreneur Awards, a national awards program that celebrates mothers in business and recognises the amazing achievements and economic contributions that mumpreneurs make to the Australian economy and in 2023 she co-founded the Women Changing The World Awards along with her sister, Peace Mitchell, and Dr Tereria Trent to recognise women making a difference around the world!

DREAM BIG; ANYTHING IS POSSIBLE!

Kelly Smeath

Melbourne, Australia, is where I live with my husband Jay, our daughter Reese and our son Brock. My life has been full of twists and turns, ups and downs.

Growing up, my parents were always hardworking and provided a wonderful home life, always there to help my brother and me navigate our way. I reflect fondly on childhood memories that were spent on weekend getaways waterskiing, relaxing on our boat in the bay and catching up with friends. During school holidays our family would pack the car for a road trip, heading north in search of warmer weather.

While sitting in the backseat of our Landcruiser, I watched through my window as the landscape changed from suburban streets and bushland to desert and onto miles of corrugated red dusty roads. During our travels, we would often see wildlife roaming in the distance in search of a waterhole and shade to escape the scorching sun. I remember the stunning sunsets in Uluru and sleeping beneath a canopy of stars lighting up the outback sky. But the highlight of these trips was meeting the resilient people of all ages living in outback remote communities and on stations across Australia.

However, the end of these adventures often meant returning to school, which I dreaded. My report cards throughout my academic years consistently noted that while I had potential, my tendency to be easily distracted and talkative resulted in mediocre grades – mostly Cs, with a few As or Bs. Academics were not my strong suit, and I struggled particularly with math and spelling, but I loved socialising, which at the time I didn't realise would come in very handy in my future pursuits.

Upon graduating from year twelve without a clear career direction, I decided to embark on an adventure in Far North Queensland and search for a job I would enjoy. It was there I started working in a media company and discovered a passion for advertising and marketing. I loved working together with business owners in rural towns to promote their products and services across Australia. This role was exhilarating and fulfilling, and I embraced every aspect of it.

Whilst I enjoyed my job, being over 2,500km away from my family and friends, I decided to move back to Melbourne to explore further opportunities in the media industry. It was during this time that I came to realise that school grades do not define one's potential or future success. What truly matters is being driven, determined and motivated; qualities that help you achieve success in all areas of life.

After a few years back in Melbourne, Jay and I were married, and we welcomed our children, Reese and Brock. Cherishing the time with my family, I made the decision to leave my job and work from home. This decision allowed me to start an online resort wear business, a venture fuelled by my love for travel.

Excited about the marketing possibilities, I reached out to Lisa Gal at Hollywood Swag Bag in the United States, proposing to feature my products in the Swag Bags given to celebrities during the award season. Seeing celebrities share posts about the gifts they received and promoting our products was exciting.

During that time, Lisa and I were in contact often, talking about various marketing ideas, even though we were in different countries we worked exceptionally well together. This gave us the idea to collaborate. It was at this time Lisa asked me to be her business partner in Australia for Hollywood Swag Bag. That way, together, we could offer businesses in Australia the opportunity to promote their products and services in the swag bags in America.

WOMEN LIVING FEARLESSLY

I accepted Lisa's offer and launched Celebrity & Hollywood Gifting, so I could also gift brands products to celebrities to celebrate red carpet events, award shows, music tours and celebrity baby announcements in Australia

Whilst also gifting nominees in America directly from Celebrity & Hollywood Gifting and Hollywood Swag Bag in honour of the Oscar, Emmy, Golden Globe and Screen Actors Guild Award weekends, showcasing products from renowned brands as well as emerging startups.

It was an opportunity I could never have predicted, but one that I embrace wholeheartedly. I never imagined I would be rubbing shoulders at events in Australia and America with some of the most influential people in the world.

To this day, I pinch myself from the young girl in high school with C grades who had no idea of what she wanted to do, to seeing my work in Hollywood. It's surreal and fills me with a sense of pride and accomplishment.

Life, however, when you least expect, has a way of slowing you down. In my early thirties I was diagnosed with skin cancer which required surgery and ongoing monitoring. This diagnosis was a reminder that life is not a rehersal and should be lived to the fullest.

During this time and reflecting, I decided I wanted to reach out to Oprah Winfrey via email. I had always watched Oprah's show and found her and her guests over the years to be very inspirational. I congratulated Oprah on the twenty-five seasons of her show and the end of an era and wished her well in the next chapter of her life.

While working one day, an email from Harpo Studios appeared in my inbox. Never thinking in a million years I would get a reply, composing myself, I opened it. To my surprise, it was an invitation to be a Skype-in guest alongside other women from around the world to be on Oprah's *Lifeclass* show on gratitude, alongside renowned figures like Deepak Chopra, Tony Robbins, Iyanla Vanzant and Bishop TD Jakes. It was a surreal experience that left me in awe, surrounded by wisdom and insight. During the show, I asked Deepak Chopra for one mantra I could take away from the *Lifeclass* show and adapt to my life immediately; his answer resonated deeply with me – 'You are your infinite potential.' This moment solidified my belief that anything is possible in life if you believe in yourself.

Life experience so far has taught me this, if you never step forward, you'll always be in the same place. That every closed door is not a setback but an opportunity to redirect and explore new paths and possibilities.

I am endlessly grateful for the love and support of my family and friends, who celebrate my successes and support me when needed. My journey has been one of resilience, creativity and unwavering determination. From challenges to building a successful business, belief in my own potential and their support has helped me achieve more than I ever thought possible.

I'm filled with gratitude for the opportunities I've been given and lessons I've learned along the way, and for the path that led Lisa and me to work together building a wonderful business and friendship.

As I look to the future, I'm excited for the doors that are yet to be opened and the adventures that await. I may not know what the future holds, but one thing's for sure; I'll meet it head-on, with my head held high and my heart full of courage, trusting in my own ability to succeed.

When you live fearlessly and dream big anything is possible.

Kelly Smeath is the owner and manager of Celebrity & Hollywood Gifting in Australia, as well as the Australian manager for Hollywood Swag Bag. With a passion for elevating brand presence on a global scale, Kelly partners with businesses worldwide to introduce their products to celebrities and influencers, thereby significantly enhancing their reach and impact in both Australia and America.

Renowned for her expertise in the gifting industry, Kelly specialises in working with brands to place their products in the gift boxes she creates that are gifted to celebrities to celebrate red carpet events, artists performing at arenas in Australia, celebrity baby announcements and other notable occasions. Her attention to detail ensures that each gift box is bespoke, reflecting the essence of the celebrated event. Collaborating with her Los Angeles based colleague, Lisa Gal at Hollywood Swag Bag, they make gift boxes and baskets brimming with products from around the world to celebrities in America during Hollywood's award season. Beyond her professional life, Kelly enjoys her frequent visits to her family's villa in Seminyak, Bali. The island's tropical climate and serene ambiance offer a perfect retreat for relaxation with friends and family creating lifelong memories. Whether dining out and exploring Bali's rich culture or simply unwinding poolside, Kelly cherishes her time on the island. This tropical paradise not only provides a peaceful escape but also serves as inspiration for her work.

Kelly's love for travel extends beyond Bali, Indonesia. Her journeys have taken her to America, Mexico, Canada, Singapore, Fiji, New Zealand, Finland, Norway and even the North Pole. Each trip enriches

KELLY SMEATH

her cultural understanding and broadens her worldview, insights that she brings back to enhance her professional pursuits. Looking ahead, Kelly aspires to explore many more countries and looks forward to collaborating with a great selection of businesses, tour operators, travel brands and accommodation partners to promote these destinations.

Kelly appreciates the coastal lifestyle of the peninsula she calls home with her husband Jay, daughter Reese, son Brock and Cavoodle Marley. The proximity to beautiful beaches, wineries, combined with weekend getaways, waterskiing and enjoying the snowfields, fills her weekends with spontaneous and enjoyable adventures.

Kelly firmly believes that hard work and dedication are essential to realising one's dreams. She has an unwavering passion for travel, loves spending time with her family and friends and is committed to creating brand awareness for the businesses that she's honoured to work with.

Website: celebrityhollywoodgifting.com.au
LinkedIn: linkedin.com/in/kelly-smeath-042865b8

CHANGING SHOES, CHANGING WORLDS

ONE MOTHER'S JOURNEY FROM BOARDROOM STILETTOS TO SNOWBOOTS DIRECTING FILMS ON CLIMATE CHANGE

Liz Courtney

'*Some people dream and wake up from their dreams. Other people dream and make their dreams their reality.*' Not many women would have hung up their stilettos for snow boots to dogsled around the Arctic North, camp on icesheets at -15°c, *without* a toilet, get lost in the heart of the Amazon jungle in the pitch-black of night and to survive a hurricane on the infamous Drake Passage in Antarctica.

But I did.

Hi, I am Liz Courtney. I used to walk the executive floors in stilettos in the advertising industry, but I traded my life of comfort to embrace a calling to direct and film one of the world's largest climate series, *The Tipping Points of Climate Change*. It didn't just happen overnight! My sliding-door moment was a few years ago, when after the successful sale of a communication and marketing agency (where I was a partner), I found the space I needed to consider … what next?

I knew I wanted to do something purposeful with my life, to make a difference, and so, concerned about the future I was leaving for my three young children,I decided to shift my writing and creative skills to film and documentaries. I wanted to focus on important stories about human endeavour and climate change. I thought *it couldn't be that hard* – just a slight step to the left!

My first documentary was a baptism of fire. While it was only a thirty-minute program, it was required in two languages! Next up, I secured a prime-time series with a different network, following a story in New York about two aspiring writers trying to launch a show on Broadway. But instead of the happy ending, it required a total pivot, like a phoenix rising from the ashes. However, when I was given the opportunity to direct a documentary in Antarctica with forty teenagers as part of the United Nations Year of Youth, my initial answer was 'no' ... Why?

I tried to trick myself. *Who would do the daily school run, pack the lunchboxes, coordinate the after-school sports schedules?* I asked myself. However, when I looked in the mirror, I realised it was my fear of the challenge, sailing the high seas across the infamous Drake Passage, that was playing with my mind. Was I going to let fear define my life? Luckily, I decided to put my fear aside to embark on this expedition, one that would go on to define my life forever. I refer to this as my sliding-door moment. And yes, we did get caught in a massive storm on the homeward leg of the Drake passage. Yes, I did call home to say I didn't think we were going to make it. Yes, waves were breaking across the bridge and over the top of the ship, as we dropped and dived 10-20m.

However, the teenagers on the enclosed bridge with the captain were not scared. They thought this wild ride through the storm was better than any ride at Disney World! I took a leaf out of their perspective, changed my viewpoint, and finally went to sleep – albeit with a seatbelt across my bed to ensure I wasn't thrown across the cabin! From this moment forward, I realised fear was really a figment of my mind. I decided to live my life, not to be controlled by fear, but to override this switch in my mind, to travel to remote locations on the planet where climate scientists were tracking and recording the pace of climate change.

My stilettos moved to a new storage area in my wardrobe, and my boot collection became quite interesting!

Following the film *Cool School Antarctica*, I developed a major six-part series, *The Tipping Points of Climate Change*, working alongside a group of brilliant climate scientists to write and direct this global series. Over four years, I explored the elements of our climate system which drive the ocean, the weather, food and water security, biodiversity and so much more, to understand what the tipping points of the climate system really are, and how close we could be to irreversible change.

WOMEN LIVING FEARLESSLY

It was a huge undertaking. Local television networks told me it was a massive series to try to get off the ground, and they doubted I could raise the funds needed. I realised that their 'no' fuelled my determination, and I headed to the US to pitch the series. With two call backs, the first major investor was confirmed. This created a domino effect, and the other seven broadcasters came onboard. This was a big achievement, raising over $2.5 million, but the gems were really in the journey. I hope my story will inspire you to move past your little voices of doubt, step out of your comfort zones, embrace the never-ending journey of self-discovery and pursue the passions that make your heart sing. But even more importantly, I encourage you to be an example for the next generation, who are going to become the *new* caretakers of our precious planet Earth.

Over the following pages, I will share the key principles that have enabled me to transform my life, embarking on new adventures while preserving what I hold dear. These principles aim to inspire and reframe the challenges, fears and limitations you might face as you step out of your current life and into the one you feel 'called to live'. I hope to invoke the fearless Walter Mitty that is in all of us!

LIFE'S TIPPING POINTS

> *'We all have many tipping points scattered in our lives. These can tip the scales for which direction we go. The key distinction here is when we have the opportunity to take it. We don't know when it'll ever come back to us.'*

For me, *Cool School Antarctica* was my sliding-door moment which led to a new world of experiences. These included meeting my adventurous self on a dogsled trekking across the Arctic in -20°. Who would have thought this city slicker, stiletto-heeled corporate executive was hiding her true self beneath this vista! There is a Walter Mitty moment in all of us, calling us to adventure. Let me share mine with you.

Qaanaaq, Greenland, 72° north, -15°c, and we are heading out towards the Arctic North Pole looking for the edge of the sea-ice to film our first episode – *The Tipping Points of the Greenland Icesheet.* A tent, a thermal mattress, snow boots on my feet and not a *real* toilet for thousands of miles. To the horizon, all we can see is flat ice. With nowhere to hide and nature calling, I realise how inconvenient it is to be female in this place. The next best option? Using collection bags for toilets. I traded my high-flying corporate job in advertising – paid a generous salary, wore shoes to die for and owned a glamour wardrobe – to experience all this!

Some might call me crazy, but I wouldn't have traded it for the world.

Travelling on the first day of our expedition, I was overcome with the realisation that I was totally at peace, amidst a sea of white glistening snow, my huskies in front of me, wind hitting my face and a film crew relying on my direction – *Wow, hello, who are you?* I asked myself.

Why, I am your adventurous self, one who has been asleep for so long. Glad to finally meet you – we have a lot of work to do to save this planet, so let's get going. My heart was racing, tingles all over my body, I realised this world is my world, it is my home and I was happy beyond words to have met my true self in the most far-flung place on the planet – the arctic sea ice in -20°c!

We travelled for hours, until we unexpectedly saw ocean, shimmering in the distance. We approached a break in the ice, called a lead and it was deemed best to run hard at the ice crack, jump with the dogs and sled across the break and land on the other side. Seemed like a plan, albeit I really had no idea because our Inuit hunters were our guides.

My sled was first to go, and I closed my eyes. We landed, and the second sled landed behind, but the dogs went crazy. The ice was moving, it was soft, like marshmallow, and in a nanosecond, I knew we were in danger.

Adrenalin rushed in and we clicked into survival mode. The Inuit guides were shouting loudly as they worked to settle the dogs and quickly turn our sleds around; the danger was apparent, and the sea ice was unstable. At any moment it could give way and we would all be facing certain death in an icy sea.

We ran the dogs hard back across the gap. In that moment there was only time to focus on getting back to safety, no time for any other thoughts or conversations with self, only the moment to be very present and very focused.

Checking everyone was okay, we stopped for a short break, some cheese and bread, and then followed the open lead for hours until we found a solid ice bridge across. Totally forgetting the sun never sets, I checked the time. Wow. At 11pm, sun high in the sky, we called it a day, set up tents, fed the dogs and made a little circle, boiling up fresh water which brought our dry-packed vegetable curries to life! Although we were all extremely tired, I had never felt more alive, living with purpose, passion, courage, kindness and a greater awareness of how we define ourselves on this planet. We discussed the film sequences for the next day and retired to our Inuit tents for the rest of the sun-drenched night.

I felt life had brought me here to witness the rare beauty of Mother Nature and record the rate of change happening at the edge of our planetary system.

The next episode was shot in the Amazon Rainforest, where our adventure started at 4am. Dressed in high-cut boots to guard me from being bitten by snakes, with my film crew, in pitch-darkness, I climbed to reach the top of a research tower which was 120m high. We were above the clouds, and above the canopies of the ancient trees. There we waited for sunrise. As the sun's glow grew in intensity, so did my feeling of *awe*. I was pinching myself, *Is this a dream?* It made the whole journey worth it. Even though I had got lost in the jungle in pitch darkness a few nights back!

I decided in my mid-forties that I did not want to live with any regrets. I wanted to find my voice, know my purpose and be of greater service – not that my busy, soccer-centric family did not come first! I needed to find my own purpose and to inspire others to step out, to have the courage to explore a wider sphere around their life.

Through my story, I hope to inspire people to take a positive view of the future. To more clearly understand the challenges and opportunities facing us this century, owing to the destabilisation of our climate system, and that together, we can work to make a difference to our own lives and our communities.

So, step out with me and take a Walter Mitty adventure that might encourage you to take risks, try new things, find another part of your amazing self, start thinking out of the box, explore change and love the new territory you find yourself in.

I hope to inspire all women seeking change and meaning in their lives to have the courage to try on new shoes which will take them on new adventures, to discover more about who they truly are and to 'live life fearlessly'. This journey often means trading an existing identity for something more meaningful. Recently, you may have taken some time out to reflect and explore what you really want to do in life. Now, it's time to act on those insights and embark on a transformative journey.

HERE ARE A FEW GUIDING PRINCIPLES TO LIVING FEARLESSLY AND WITH PURPOSE

NO MEANS GO
Choosing your adventures in life, despite what others think you ought or ought not to do, is vital. It is never too late; it is never too outrageous … and it is worth it. You are worth it!

TAKE THEIR LOVE, NOT THEIR ADVICE
When stepping out, you might face criticism for being irresponsible. Friends and family do this because it challenges their status quo. It is

not always ill-intended, but if you are stepping out, you must be aware of this.

CHANGING WORLDS
You might start to feel alien to your friendship circles because your adventures and way of living are far out of their realities. While others might focus on weekly leisure activities, your pursuits will be different – and that's okay.

SEEING 'AND' RATHER THAN 'OR'
Balancing multiple roles can seem impossible. For me, I couldn't see how I could effectively be both an adventure film director and a mother and partner simultaneously. But I learned to integrate these roles, rather than choosing one over the other.

FEAR MASKED AS DUTY
I used my duty as a mother as an excuse not to go on adventures. But I realised it was all fear. My children were supportive of what I wanted, as was my husband.

HAVE A CHAT, DON'T GUESS
Sometimes the best way to know for sure is to ask or have a chat with someone about it. I was worried about my children, but they encouraged me to go on my adventures.

IT'S NEVER TOO LATE
I was in my forties when I declared a change. It's never too late to step out, embrace adventure and live the life you feel called to live. Many of us find ourselves at a crossroads, excelling professionally, yet feeling unfulfilled inside. We often grapple with the decision of whether to continue our current path or finally make the significant change we always contemplate during our spare moments.

As women we have frequently sacrificed our true passions for the sake of security or to meet other obligations. However, many of us seek answers to some of life's most profound questions:
- What am I supposed to do?
- Why am I going through all this?
- Why are we even here?
- Is this all there is?

Days filled with responsibilities leave us with only fleeting moments for ourselves, feeling that we need permission to pursue our true desires, despite having a unique perspective on life and spirituality. We often keep these thoughts to ourselves, hesitant to voice them publicly. I know this because it was me before I overcame my fear, jumped through that sliding-door moment in my life, and decided to live a life with a greater purpose – to live fearlessly.

FINAL WORDS

When you step out to create your dreams, the steps to get there can be hazy. However, being able to sit in the space of not knowing is important. It challenges you, keeps you on edge and helps you learn what you need to learn to fulfil your vision. You are never given a challenge unworthy of your human spirit.

LIZ COURTNEY

Liz Courtney is an award-winning international film director, with over fifty-five documentaries to her slate of projects, primarily around climate change, sustainable solutions and youth engagement, to drive action and hope. In 2024, Liz was recognised at the Women Changing the World Awards in London, for her work in media, driving awareness and education around climate change, is a finalist in this years Womens Agenda Climate Hero Award, and has been awarded 100 Women of Influence in Australia and inducted into the Australian Business Women's Hall of Fame.

She has produced and directed one of the largest series on climate change, *The Tipping Points*, working with leading climate scientists, uniquely engaged with the IPCC, on writing and directing *Earth's Survival – Decoding the Climate Report*, and took up the prestigious role as artist in residence at the Earth Observatory of Singapore at NTU University in 2019. Here Liz has made several award-winning programs including *Climate Impact Asia*, *Changing Oceans*, *Future Cities Asia*, a special anime short series for youth called *Earth Girl's Mission*, and her most recent feature documentary, *Antarctica the Giant Awakens*. In 2023, Liz wrote and directed the daily youth program at COP28 in Dubai and was co-founder of Youth4Planet in Europe.

Liz has spoken internationally (Singapore, Indonesia, Hong Kong, London, Vienna, New York and Australia), sharing her inspirational story and educating the audience to understand climate change through the eyes of the next generation. Currently Liz is presenting *Antarctica the Giant Awakens* around the world, developing a new animation series for three to five years on climate change titled *Adventure Bunny's Big Little Adventures* and gearing up for *The Positive Tipping Points* documentary series in 2025.

FEARLESSLY EMBRACING LIFE'S OPPORTUNITIES

Lisa Gal

STEPPING FORWARD

Life is interesting in the way that sometimes the opportunities that present themselves are not something one has sought out particularly. It is an opportunity that has risen from the strengths and talents a person has, coupled with the perfect opportunity presented at the 'perfect' time! It is all about timing. I think when these things happen, life is energetically telling you, *This is what you NEED to be doing.*

I graduated from UCLA in 1996 with a degree in business. Still unsure of the path I wanted to take, I took a job at a production company, and I wanted to work in the wardrobe department so I was aiming towards that goal, doing whatever I could to try and make that happen. Life had a different plan for me as I was moving along on paths that held no interest, and I was moving farther from the goal I had set for myself. One day the entire production company shut down and I was faced with the question, *What do I do now?*

That answer came from a friend who saw the gift baskets I was making for the ad agencies (a side job on set) coming into town for production, and he stated I should start my own gift basket business. Thus, Hollywood Baskets was born in 1997. Back then not many people had websites and the friend that told me to open a gift basket business also told me he would build me a website. It was so incredibly exciting when one day I received a call from someone in another state wanting to order a gift from me. I felt so ahead of the curve as far as Internet sales were concerned.

I was based in Burbank CA and built up such amazing clientele from the studios to five-star hotels. The list goes on and on. One of my big accounts was The Four Seasons Hotel in Beverly Hills. One day I received a call from the GM. He was frantic. He told me he had a big magazine vendor who used to make gift bags for the talent during awards season (Golden Globe Awards, Grammy's, Oscars and Emmys) and that after budget cuts, they would no longer be able to service the hotel with these bags. He was wondering if I could do gifts for the nominees.

Thus came a HUGE dilemma. The hotel was not willing to pay me for these gift baskets.

I made a few calls, and a friend told me that there were resources on the Internet where I could ask for luxury products to place into my baskets. It sounded great BUT I wasn't making any money. In any event, I decided to go for it. I made my first baskets for Oscar nominees staying at the hotel in 2007. It was a HUGE hit! The talent was overwhelmed with the amazing products I gifted them in a beautifully curated gift basket. There were nominees taking photos of their baskets and posting them on Instagram and Twitter. I was floored. Only a moment away was my great opportunity, which had so much to do with TIMING! The woman who used to do the gift bags for the magazine I mentioned saw my gift baskets and asked the hotel who prepared them. They gave her my number and the rest is history. She reached out to me letting me know she had advertisers that were willing to pay top dollar to participate in the gift baskets for the nominees. We formed a partnership and began gifting all the awards shows with the hotel.

Enter Kelly Smeath, my amazing partner in this publication. Kelly was a client who placed her own products in my gift baskets all the way from Australia. She enjoyed the process and reached out to me about working together. She told me she had many brands in Australia that were incredibly interested in placing their products in these gift baskets and our partnership was formed. We have worked together since 2009 and have grown together in this amazing business. We have had the opportunities to gift Oprah, Ellen DeGeneres, the Royal family and

WOMEN LIVING FEARLESSLY

all the amazing nominees through the years. Our gifting continues to thrive, and we plan on expanding our business to Singapore and Dubai. The press and media our brands have received has been incredible. We have together been featured in *People* magazine, *Fortune* magazine, *Access Hollywood*, *Extra*, *CNN*, *Forbes* and more.

The sky is the limit if you let these opportunities enter when you least expect it and roll with it. I currently live in Los Angeles with my three children and husband.

I am blessed.

Lisa Gal, a prominent figure in Hollywood, has carved a unique niche as the owner of Hollywood Baskets since 1999 and Hollywood Swag Bag since 2007. Her journey into the entertainment industry began after graduating from UCLA's School of Business in 1996, where she honed her business acumen and developed a passion for supporting actors in achieving their dreams.

Known for her boundless energy and dedication, Lisa has become a respected talent manager, representing notable clients such as Kathy Garver, Billy Hufsey and Trevor Larcom. Her expertise extends beyond talent management; she has also contributed as a casting associate for several productions, leveraging her insider knowledge to help shape the industry's landscape.

Lisa's entrepreneurial spirit and keen eye for opportunities led her to establish Hollywood Baskets and Hollywood Swag Bag, through which she procures and curates gift bags for prestigious events like the Oscars, Emmys, Golden Globes and Grammy's. Partnering closely with The Four Seasons Hotel in Beverly Hills, she has orchestrated memorable gifting experiences that have earned her recognition in *People* magazine, *Forbes* magazine, *Fortune* magazine, *CNN* and other esteemed publications.

Beyond her entrepreneurial ventures, Lisa is passionate about giving back to her community. She founded the Swag Gives Back Program, which allows celebrities to contribute to charitable causes through her platforms, notably partnering with LA Family Housing to support vulnerable populations.

In addition to her thriving career, Lisa is embarking on a new chapter

LISA GAL

as an author. Collaborating with her Australian counterpart and other inspiring women, she is co-authoring the book *Women Living Fearlessly*, set to launch in NYC in October. This venture reflects her commitment to empowering women and sharing stories of courage and resilience.

Lisa Gal continues to innovate and inspire in the entertainment industry, embodying a blend of business savvy, creative vision and philanthropic spirit. Her impact reaches far beyond Hollywood, leaving an indelible mark on both the entertainment world and the community she serves.

Website: hollywoodbaskets.com & hollywoodswagbag.com
LinkedIn: linkedin.com/in/lisa-gal-b488207

FEAR = FALSE EVIDENCE APPEARING REAL

Mafae Yunon - Belasco

In the chronicles of time, women have continuously shown the world what it means to live fearlessly. This chapter is dedicated to every woman who has dared to step out of the shadows, break societal norms and carve her own path. This is my story.

From a young age, I was taught to be obedient, quiet and compliant. Growing up in a 'Filipino' culture where traditions were deeply rooted, the expectations placed upon me were clear: follow the rules, don't ask questions and certainly don't challenge the status quo. But deep within me, there was a fire that refused to be extinguished. The first significant leap towards living fearlessly came when I decided to pursue the field of hospitality and tourism education. It wasn't a popular decision among my family and community, as the Filipino culture is known to be guided in the medical, engineering or law field, but I knew that knowledge and passion was my key to freedom. Completing my degree and working in a vibrant city (Sydney, Australia), I was exposed to a world of ideas and opportunities I had never imagined. Here, I learned the value of my voice and the strength of my convictions.

Graduating college was just the beginning. I chose a career in a male-dominated field (being a chef); a decision met with skepticism and doubt. The whispers of, *Can she handle it?* and, *Isn't this too much for a woman?* only fuelled my determination. I faced challenges head-on, proving not just to others, but to myself, that I was capable.

Living fearlessly isn't about the absence of fear, it's about standing tall despite it. The kitchen world was a battlefield, and there were days when I felt overwhelmed. But every setback was a lesson, every failure a stepping stone. I surrounded myself with mentors and allies, women and men who believed in gender equality and empowerment. This then led me to a bigger goal: representing my country. Playing tennis, starting at the age of nine, taught me the qualities of being responsible for my own actions, accountability and independence. I have always dreamt of making it to the Olympics or major tournaments, where I would compete with other countries. Sure enough, the stars were aligned for me, for the Miss World Pageant 2003. Yes! A pageant led me to the dreams of representing my country as Miss World Philippines 2003.

As I climbed the ladder of success, I made a promise to myself: I would help others rise – most importantly, women. I started mentoring young women, sharing my story and encouraging them to relentlessly pursue their dreams. Together, we created a network of support, a sisterhood of warriors ready to face the world. My strong faith has played a huge part in every life experience I've encountered up to today.

Philippians 4:6 – 'Don't worry about anything; instead, pray about everything. Tell God what you need and thank him for all he has done.' Philippians 4:13 – 'For I can do everything through Christ, who gives me strength.' Beyond my professional achievements, living fearlessly also meant embracing my true self. I challenged societal norms in my personal life, advocating for mental health, body positivity and self-love. I learned that true courage lies in authenticity, in being unapologetically yourself.

What you think becomes what you say. What you say becomes what you do. What you do becomes your habit. Your habit becomes your second nature, and your second nature becomes your character. Becoming the fearless woman I am comes with positive habits such as these and it starts with the mindset. Be mindful of your thoughts.

'Women living fearlessly' is a testament to the resilience, strength and indomitable spirit of women everywhere. My story is but one thread in the rich tapestry of fearless women. Together, we are a force to be reckoned with, lighting the way for future generations.

MAFAE YUNON-BELASCO

Maria Rafaela 'Mafae' Yunon-Belasco is best known for her success in the beauty pageant industry, having won prestigious awards locally and internationally, such as Miss Philippines Australia 1998, Binibining Pilipinas World 2003 (and prominently landing top five in the Miss World competition of the same year held in Sanya, China), and Mrs Philippines Globe 2008.

She has since gone on to channel her expertise into image consulting for Binibinig Pilipinas (Miss Philippines Pageant) since 2003, taking on the role of personality development director for the Miss World Philippines in 2021 and pageant director of kumu Global Pageants on the number-one livestreaming app of the Philippines, kumu. She continued on her journey in expanding her services and entrepreneur expertise, starting up her own company – Mafae Management Consultancy (founded 2015), wherein she manages talents, spearheads public relations and marketing, content creation, events management, online show production and social media management for companies and individuals all over the world.

Mafae has vast experience in commercial, ramp and print modelling, and even television and events hosting. She enjoys passing on her knowledge of each of her experiences through her talks, workshops and shows which she does on a weekly basis. She is firm in her mission of making the world a brighter space as a certified life and personality development coach, sacred space holder and wellbeing boost facilitator where she helps others become their best selves through positive mindset guidance.

Mafae, alongside her husband Nic Belasco, former professional basketball player in the PBA (Philippine Basketball Association), also owns

MAFAE YUNON - BELASCO

a sports academy – the Belasco Unlimited Skills Academy where she coaches tennis. Mafae is passionate about empowering others with her family campaign #SaveLivesOnline, where she encourages others to be their true and authentic selves online while populating the digital world with positive content.

Awarded 100 Most Influential Filipino Women on LinkedIn 2021, took on the roles of Australia regional director and kumu Creators Academy Head for kumu number-one livestreaming app in the Philippines. Recently, she was appointed marketing and PR director of Bolo Music Group and president of Filipino American National Historical Society Stockton, California USA Chapter.

Mafae lives by her motto 'the world is yours' and 'time + productivity = success', and aims to bring the best out of everyone around her.

Lastly, the biggest reward in her life is being a mum, bringing up her own young leaders of today in her six children, Nico, Mike, Moses, Nicole, Noah and Melo. To add the cherry on top is her husband Nic, who supports and mentors Mafae in all that she does.

Instagram: instagram.com/mafaeyunonbelasco
LinkedIn: linkedin.com/in/mafae-yunon-belasco
YouTube: youtube.com/@mafaemanagementconsultancy3567
Website: mafaemanagement.com

COURAGE ACROSS CONTINENTS

TALES OF RESILIENCE

Mercedes Soria

FROM ECUADOR TO THE LAND OF DREAMS

I wasn't supposed to be 'much'. I was born and raised in Ambato, Ecuador – a third-world country where people keep their cars for twenty years and only dream of buying a house with their entire life savings.

I am the daughter of a single mother who, at the time, only had a high school degree and no education beyond that. But you see, I had a massive advantage over everyone else; I was born with an identical twin sister, her name was Pauli. I would never know how much of an advantage this was until I turned forty-six years old. More on this later.

The three of us were a small, close-knit family, and I was loved. We never knew what it was to be rich, so we never knew that *not having money* wasn't ideal. We were happy with the life our mother gave us: full of love, discipline and dreams. She always told us that the sky was the limit, and throughout this story, I will reveal the secrets she taught us that have enabled me to be in the privileged position I am today and to live my life fearlessly!

Mother went on to study, getting a PhD and becoming president of her school. This story is about her lessons and teachings, and how you can apply them to get whatever you want out of life.

The most a person like me could hope for, back home, was to be a bank teller. Yes, if you were smart and studied hard (and possibly being beautiful was a massive plus), you could aspire to work for *Banco del Pacifico*, the country's biggest bank. At least that is what my dad always said, but my mother had more in mind. She had dreams, and *she always pushed us to be good students and taught us a love for reading books and the importance of working hard – Mother's lesson #1.*

Pauli and I were not liked much, in either primary school or high school, just because we were the girls who always had the best grades. It seems many people didn't like that, but we didn't care, we had each other. We gave our studies everything we had. *Success depends on the actions and steps you take to achieve it, and building good habits is essential – Mother's lesson #2.*

Despite being very poor, I always felt a pull towards something greater, a desire to seek opportunities that just weren't available back home. It was this ambition that led Pauli and me to make the difficult decision to immigrate to the United States. Leaving our mother and everything familiar behind was incredibly hard, but we were determined to create a better future for ourselves.

TRIALS AND TRIBULATIONS IN A NEW WORLD

With a scholarship to Middle Tennessee State University, we arrived in the United States and quickly realised that starting a new life was going to be much harder than we had anticipated, since we didn't speak the language! We faced a culture shock and the overwhelming feeling of being homesick was a constant companion. If Pauli had not come with me, I believe it would have been impossible to be where I am today; I would have gone back to Ecuador. Finding stable employment was another significant challenge, and we had to adapt quickly to a new social and cultural environment. But Pauli and I had each other and that was enough. Despite the hurdles and the immigration process being particularly stressful, giving up was never an option for us. *Learn to fend for yourself and you will make it anywhere – Mother's lesson #3.*

OVERCOMING ADVERSITY WITH GRIT

The legal challenges I faced in securing residency were some of the toughest times in my life. The process was long, expensive and emotionally draining. But my determination saw me through. I often worked multiple jobs (painting, graveyard shifts, McDonald's, etc.) while attending school to make ends meet. We didn't have much, even having to split our meals in half so we could both eat something. Each obstacle I overcame only strengthened my resolve. My journey was far from easy, but every step forward felt like a victory, no matter what … you keep going!

I had a nearly flawless record in school, graduating with the highest honour one could get, but even so, I applied to over a hundred companies after graduating with a master's degree in computer science, and was only offered one job that would allow me to stay in the US, but that was all I needed! *You will find success only through sheer grit and determination, facing every obstacle head-on and refusing to back down – Mother's lesson #4.*

BUILDING A FEARLESS FUTURE

Once I secured my legal status, I focused on building a successful career in the tech industry. My hard work paid off as I started to achieve significant milestones and gain recognition for my contributions. I was the person who kept her eyes open for more 'things to get involved in'. Not because I wanted to get something out of my involvement, but because the more I worked, the more I noticed my values were changing. While at the beginning of my career, I wanted to be the best at my job to keep climbing the corporate ladder. As time passed, I discovered that helping others was more fulfilling than having the top job. I mentored several women at Deloitte (a professional services company with 200,000 employees worldwide) to help them get better jobs in tech. I was the founder of the Deloitte Hispanic Network which we called HNet! (How original, no?) I was also involved in the women's network and was a part of the diversity and inclusion board at Deloitte. *Values change with age and that is okay, change is good – Mother's lesson #5.*

I became involved in my community, advocating for immigrant rights and mentoring others who were going through similar experiences. It felt incredibly rewarding to give back and support others on their journey. I started to be recognised for my work, receiving awards like the Top 40 under 40 in Tennessee.

It's important to note that I had always lived with my sister. For thirty-six years, we were never separated and that was the way we liked it. She was the wind beneath my wings, the one to always celebrate my successes and tell the world about me. She supported every crazy project I had, from fundraisers to having mariachis at work celebrating Cinco de Mayo. She thought I was nuts for getting involved in so many things, but she supported me all the way. In her eyes, I could do no wrong. She loved me unconditionally.

Marrying my husband meant moving away from my sister. When I came to Silicon Valley to start a company with him, I was lost in an uncomfortable stage in my life when my old self was gone. I was trying to figure out what my new self was going to be. *Being lost is okay, that means you are evolving, look forward to your new self, growing is good – Mother's lesson #6.*

Once Knightscope was up and running, I started my involvement in other activities, which my sister called 'extracurricular activities'. I joined the United Nations Association of the United States, where I learned about the work of the United Nations and even participated in the global summit.

I was awarded the Silicon Valley Women of Influence award in 2017 and also the AnitaB.org Grace Hopper award for leadership due to the work I was doing helping women in tech and STEM careers. By this time, I had decided that what I wanted to do was help women, and I also wanted to do more travelling. I had no idea how I would merge both, but God had a plan for me.

Travelling? That is new, you say. Yes, this is how it happened.

While I was at Deloitte I was asked to participate in recruiting events, especially for Latino conferences. I was super excited, as I wanted more Latino men and women to not only have jobs but to succeed in careers in STEM. During those trips I got to know many cities around the United States, and I always enjoyed the trips; meeting new people, engaging with them and even making their dreams come true by interviewing them on the spot and helping them secure employment. *Always help others as much as you can, that is what matters. If you help others, someone might help you when you are in need – Mother's lesson #7.*

A CHANCE ENCOUNTER

I have a friend in Silicon Valley who was asked to join a casting session for a show that would be called *The Real Housewives of Silicon Valley*. She was apprehensive, so she asked me to go with her. The show did not get made but I met a woman there and we struck up a conversation. She mentioned, 'If you love helping women you should be involved in TechWomen.' I asked what that was and she said, 'The US State Department brings women from all over the world here to Silicon Valley to be coached by executive women, to help them start their businesses.' This sounded like the perfect thing for me to get involved with and to take my impact outside of the United States to the rest of the world. I signed up immediately! *When an opportunity presents itself to you, you never know if it will be the one to change your life. Stay on the lookout always – Mother's lesson #8.*

I was accepted as an executive mentor for the program, and I have coached women from Tunisia, Lebanon, Algeria, Morocco and many other countries. I have loved every minute of it. Learning about them, their culture, what is important to them and how we can support one of their local programs with technology. For one of the projects, we created a summer STEM camp for teenagers in Tunisia.

One day, out of the blue, I received a call from Washington DC. It was a representative of the United States Department of State who said I'd been referred to them by the TechWomen team as someone who should be a part of the US speaker program. Basically, I would travel the world and represent the US State Department, giving speeches about entrepreneurship, artificial intelligence (my field), innovation and women in STEM.

I hesitated taking this on at first; my plate was full with work and those 'extracurricular activities' I am known for. But after my shock at the news, I discussed this with Pauli who was born to travel. She loved it and said, 'What? The US Federal Government asks you to represent them, and you're going to say no? Are you crazy?' She was a big influence on me, and it was five years ago when I accepted the assignment.

I loved to go to the conferences, schools, incubators, press briefings and other events I spoke at. For all these events, Pauli travelled with me. I distinctly remember a talk I did in Mexico when one of the questions from the audience was, 'What is the motor that propels you to accomplish so much?' (Literal translation from Spanish but you get the idea). I did not hesitate for a minute and my answer was, 'Two women. One is right here in the first row, my twin sister Pauli, and the second is my mother in South America. Everything I do is to make them both proud.' It is the truth, and it will always be that way.

Unfortunately, at forty-six years old, my beloved sister passed away unexpectedly. While I am grieving every night, still, I have somehow learned to do things on my own. I would have loved more time with her, but I still have the same motivation to live my life to the fullest; to make her proud. *The people who love you will always be with you, even if it is not in person – Mother's lesson #9.*

Recently, I won an award at the Women Changing the World Awards for my work with women in STEM around the world. To this day, this work has impacted over 25,000 women and counting. I received my award in London and got to meet Sarah Ferguson, Duchess of York. *Boy, has my life changed from being that poor kid in Ecuador!* I said to myself.

Even though I was dreading the trip alone without Pauli, I managed to enjoy it very much and I know she is proud of me. Do you know how I know? Because as I was receiving my award, they played one of Pauli's most favourite songs. What a sign!

I checked my LinkedIn page recently and saw that, in my career, I have received over twenty awards. It only matters because my mother is proud, and Pauli is too. I was able to do this due to my 'extracurricular activities'. It is important to get involved with others, to give back; it just makes the world a better place in my opinion. It is never about the award itself, it is always about the experience you had that took you there.

One piece of advice I would give you is to talk to people who are older than you and who have lived a good life. Ask them how it was? What did they do? What ended up being the most important part of their lives? Also, what are they not proud of? Sometimes we get caught up in our daily little problems and forget we have the privilege of this life and therefore have the responsibility to live it to the fullest.

EMPOWERING OTHERS: MY MESSAGE TO THE WORLD

Looking back, my life story is one of overcoming immense adversity to achieve success. I share my experiences to hopefully inspire you, showing you that fearlessness is something you cultivate through persistence and resilience. I want you to know that you can embrace challenges and persevere through hardships, just as I did. If I could navigate the turbulent waters of immigration and build a successful life starting from nothing, so can you.

My journey is proof that with determination and courage, anything is possible and that you will get enormous satisfaction by helping others. So, go out and do what makes you happy, help others and even if you are afraid to try, do it anyway … be FEARLESS!

Mercedes is a technologist who joined Deloitte as a senior software engineer leading the knowledge management team. She worked with the most cutting-edge technologies. She was the only female in a team of forty people. She was quickly promoted to manager and then channel leader for ethics and compliance. Her role involved leading engineering teams to work on applications that were used by over 200,000 people around the world with an up time requirement of 99.999%. She then focused on large-scale deployments of human resources, ethics, compliance, financial and product development enterprise tools.

Mercedes has two bachelor's and a master's degree in computer science in addition to an executive MBA and certificates from MIT and Harvard Business School. She truly believes that technology plays an important role in business success.

Mercedes has a passion for inspiring and leading women in technology. She mentored dozens of women while at Deloitte. She was member of the Women in Technology Council and board member for the diversity and inclusion initiatives at Deloitte where she affected change to ensure more diversity. She was the founder of the first Hispanic Network at Deloitte. She was also member of the Society of Professional Engineers.

She was invited to join the TechWomen program from the state department which aims to teach, mentor and educate women in STEM from Africa, the Middle East and Asia. Only distinguished women are invited and even less get approved to participate and she got in. Her project with the Tunisian team was winner of founding dollars during the evaluation period. She is a true mentor and advisor to women's technology projects not just in the USA but around the world. She firmly believes that the true potential of women in technology has not been reached yet, there is much to do still, and she has been and is willing to put in the work.

She is equally comfortable working in startups. From Carbon Motors to Knightscope, she flourished in the startup ecosystem and was promoted to director of information technology, EVP and then C-level titles like chief intelligence officer and chief information security officer.

At Knightscope she leads the engineering team tasked with building the company's core software product, the Knightscope security operations centre. This application collects data that autonomous robots ingest and present to the customer in a way that can be understood and acted upon. The technology stack involves artificial intelligence, machine learning, computer vision, cloud and web technologies.

She has received more than twenty awards in her career. Many due to her involvement with women in tech organisations, the United States State Department, United Nations Association of the USA and the Forbes Women Forum.

She has been awarded the Silicon Valley Women of Influence award and the Women Changing the World award which she received in London.

She deeply believes that there is much more women potential that has not been tapped into yet; she will continue her work to get it done.

FROM SHADOWS TO SPOTLIGHT

Patricia Gonde

FROM THE CRADLE TO THE STAGE: A WOMAN'S JOURNEY TO AUTHENTICITY

From infancy, I was nurtured in a world dominated by masculine authority. As a daughter, wife and professional, my roles were predetermined, their scripts meticulously outlined by societal norms and familial expectations. The weight of these expectations often felt suffocating, a heavy cloak that muffled my authentic voice. Growing up in a patriarchal society, I learned to navigate a labyrinth of limitations, my spirit often confined to the shadows. Yet, within the depths of this constrained existence, a flicker of defiance ignited, a spark that would eventually illuminate my path to authenticity.

This journey, from timid acquiescence to fearless assertion, has been a tapestry woven with threads of resilience, determination and an unwavering belief in the power of the human spirit. It is a story of overcoming, of rising, of daring to be different.

THE WEIGHT OF EXPECTATIONS

I grew up in a world painted in pastel hues. As a girl, my canvas was pre-coloured, the strokes defined by societal norms and familial expectations. A daughter, first and foremost, my role was etched in bold strokes: obedient, respectful, a silent admirer of the men in my world. My father, a towering figure in our small village, cast a long shadow. His expectations were like the sun warming me when met, scorching when defied. A doctor, he envisioned for me, a life cloaked in white, a path as predictable as the sunrise.

The world whispered its own set of rules. A woman's worth was measured by her ability to nurture, to be a dutiful wife, a loving mother. Ambition was a foreign language, a word whispered with caution. Marriage was the grand finale, the ultimate achievement. Love, it was said, conquered all, including self-doubt.

I was a puppet on invisible strings, dancing to a melody not my own. My heart, a silent orchestra, played a different tune. Yet, fear was the conductor, stifling the symphony of my soul. The fear of disappointing, of being ostracised, kept me trapped in a gilded cage.

With each passing year, the dissonance grew louder. The girl who loved to dissect flowers, to question the why of the world, was being muffled by the woman society expected. I yearned to explore, to dream, to reach for the stars, but the weight of expectations was a leaden anchor.

It was in the quiet moments, lost in the pages of books, that I found solace. Authors became my confidants, their worlds a refuge from my confines. In their stories, I discovered women who defied norms, who dared to dream. They ignited a spark, a flicker of hope that perhaps, just perhaps, I too could rewrite my script.

The pressure was relentless, a constant undercurrent in my life. The unspoken rules were as rigid as the iron gates that enclosed our family compound. To question the status quo was akin to blasphemy. To voice an opinion that differed from the patriarchal norm was to invite scorn. I learned to bite my tongue, to suppress my thoughts, to become a silent observer of my own life.

The weight of these expectations was not merely a psychological burden; it was a physical one as well. It manifested as a tightness in my chest, a heaviness in my limbs. I felt trapped, a bird with clipped wings, yearning for the freedom of flight.

There were moments of rebellion, fleeting flashes of defiance, but they were quickly extinguished by the fear of consequences. To challenge the status quo meant risking the love and approval of those I cherished. It was a terrifying prospect. I was a chameleon, adapting to my environment, changing colour to blend in. I lost myself in the process, becoming a reflection of the expectations projected onto me.

As Maya Angelou wisely said, 'I learned that people will forget what you said, people will forget what you did, but people will never forget how you made them feel.' It was time to stop being a silent observer and start crafting my own story. It was time to step out of the shadows and into the spotlight.

THE AWAKENING

The weight of expectation was a heavy cloak, suffocating my spirit. Yet, within the depths of this imposed silence, a flicker of rebellion began to stir. It was a tiny spark, a whisper against the gale-force winds of conformity.

The women in the books I read ignited a fire within me, a longing to break free from expectations. I started to question the unspoken rules, to challenge the status quo. It was a terrifying journey, like a moth drawn to a flame, drawn to a life beyond the confines of my prescribed role. I began to see the world through a different lens. The pink and blue hues faded, replaced by a spectrum of possibilities. I realised my worth was not determined by my ability to conform, but by my capacity to create. The fear of failure was a formidable opponent, but the desire for authenticity was a stronger force.

It was a slow, arduous process. Every step away from the expected path was met with resistance. Family, friends and even strangers questioned my choices. I was labelled as rebellious, arrogant, even ungrateful. But I pressed on, fuelled by a growing belief in myself. I discovered the power of silence. In a world that demands constant noise, I found strength in solitude. In these quiet moments, I connected with my inner self, discovering a resilience I never knew existed. I learned to trust my intuition, to listen to the whispers of my heart.

The journey was fraught with challenges, but it was also a journey of self-discovery. I began to understand that true strength lies not in conforming but in defying expectations, embracing our uniqueness, celebrating differences and living a life aligned with our passions.

It was time to make people feel inspired, to show them that it's possible to break free from the chains of expectation and live a life of purpose and authenticity.

I remember a quote by Ralph Waldo Emerson that resonated with me during this time: 'The only person you are destined to become is the person you decide to be.' It was a powerful reminder that my future was in my hands. I was the architect of my destiny, and it was time to start building.

The road ahead was uncertain, filled with twists and turns. But with each step, I grew stronger, more confident. I realised that fear was a formidable opponent, but it was not invincible. I could choose to let it paralyse me, or I could choose to use it as fuel for my journey. As Nelson Mandela wisely said, 'It always seems impossible until it's done.' And so, I took the first step, and then the next, and the next. With every challenge I faced, I emerged stronger, more resilient. I was becoming the woman I was meant to be.

BREAKING FREE

The shackles of expectation clanged around me; a constant reminder of the boundaries imposed. Yet, within the depths of my soul, a fire ignited, a determination to break free. I began to question the narratives that had been scripted for me. Was my worth defined by societal roles or by my potential? Could I rewrite the ending to my story?

The journey to liberation was fraught with challenges. There were days when doubt crept in, whispering tales of failure. But I refused to be a prisoner of fear. I embraced discomfort as a catalyst for growth, understanding that every challenge was an opportunity to learn and evolve.

I sought out mentors, women who had broken free from the mould. Their stories inspired me, their wisdom guided me. I joined forces with like-minded individuals, creating a support network that fuelled my ambition. Together, we challenged stereotypes, shattered glass ceilings and redefined success.

The workplace was a battleground, a terrain dominated by masculine energy, but I refused to be intimidated. I learned to assert myself without being aggressive, to negotiate without compromising my values. I discovered the power of my voice and used it to advocate for myself and others. It was a long and arduous journey, filled with setbacks, as well as triumphs. There were moments of exhilaration and moments of profound doubt. Through it all, I held onto my vision of a life lived on my own terms.

I learned that true strength is not about overpowering others, but about standing tall in one's own truth. It's about finding your voice, using it with courage, and inspiring others to do the same. As Eleanor Roosevelt once said, 'No-one can make you feel inferior without your consent.' I refused to give my consent. I was determined to create a life that was not just about survival, but about thriving. I wanted to leave a legacy, to inspire generations of women to reach for their full potential. It was a daunting task, but one I embraced with unwavering determination.

FORGING MY PATH

With each shattered chain of expectation, a new path unfolded. The woman I was becoming was a mosaic of resilience, determination and unwavering belief in myself. I realised my journey was not about reaching a destination, but about relishing the process of becoming.

The world often tried to categorise me, to fit me into predetermined boxes. But I refused to be labelled. I was a kaleidoscope of experiences, emotions and aspirations. I embraced the complexity, the contradictions, the imperfections that made me uniquely human.

I learned the power of vulnerability. Sharing my story, my fears and my triumphs, I discovered a profound connection with others. In the tapestry of human experience, we are all intricately woven together. By sharing our stories, we create a safety net, a community where we can support and uplift one another.

Leadership, I discovered, is not about wielding power but about empowering others. It's about creating a space where everyone feels valued, where differences are celebrated and where collaboration thrives. I became a mentor, a guide, a beacon of hope for those who dared to dream. There were times when the weight of responsibility felt overwhelming. The imposter syndrome crept in, whispering doubts in my ear. But I reminded myself of the journey I had traversed, the battles I had won. I was not a victim of circumstance, but a creator of my reality.

I learned to balance ambition with compassion, to lead with empathy and to serve with humility. I understood that true success is not measured by wealth or status, but by the impact we make on the world. It was a journey of self-discovery, of finding my voice and of claiming my space in the world. I was no longer a silent observer; I was an active participant in shaping my destiny and the destiny of others.

As the poet Rupi Kaur beautifully penned, 'You are the sum of all the storms you have weathered.' I had weathered many storms and emerged stronger, wiser and more determined than ever.

INSPIRING CHANGE

I had broken free from the chains of expectation, but the journey was far from over. With new-found freedom came a responsibility; to inspire others to follow their own paths. I realised my story was not just about personal liberation, but about creating a ripple effect of change.

I began to share my experiences, speaking at conferences, workshops and schools. My voice, once silenced, became a powerful tool for empowerment. I shared the blueprint of my journey, offering hope and inspiration to those who felt trapped in their own gilded cages.

I founded organisations dedicated to empowering women, providing them with the tools and resources to reach their full potential. I mentored young girls, igniting in them a spark of ambition. I became a champion for equality, advocating for policies that supported women's advancement.

It was not always easy. There were detractors, those who questioned my motives, who doubted my ability to effect change. But I persevered, fuelled by a vision of a world where women were not just tolerated but celebrated. I learned the importance of collaboration. Together with like-minded individuals, we created a powerful force for change. We shattered glass ceilings, redefined leadership and created a more inclusive world. I embraced the role of a catalyst, igniting the spark of potential in others.

To see the impact of my work on the lives of others was the ultimate fulfilment. I had gone from being a silent observer to a catalyst for change, and that, in itself, was a revolution.

I had done what would have previously felt impossible to me. I had broken free, found my voice and inspired others to do the same. My story was no longer just mine; it was a shared narrative, a testament to the power of the human spirit.

CONQUERING CHALLENGES

The path to liberation is rarely smooth. It is paved with obstacles, detours and unexpected storms. From imposter syndrome to work-life balance, women face a unique set of challenges that can be overwhelming. Yet, within these challenges lie opportunities for growth and resilience.

Imposter syndrome, the insidious doubt that creeps in despite accomplishments, is a common experience for women in leadership. It's the whisper that questions your abilities, telling you that you don't belong.

But remember, you earned your place. Your skills and experience are valid. Celebrate your achievements and surround yourself with supportive people who believe in you.

Work-life balance is another formidable challenge. The relentless demands of career and family can be exhausting. It's essential to set boundaries, prioritise tasks and delegate when possible. Self-care is not selfish; it's a necessity. Recharge your batteries through activities you enjoy, whether it's spending time in nature, practicing yoga or simply indulging in a good book.

Dealing with criticism can be bruising, especially for women. It's important to distinguish between constructive feedback and personal attacks. Focus on the substance of the criticism, not the delivery. Learn to set boundaries and disengage from toxic relationships. Not everyone will agree with you, and that's okay.

Resilience is the cornerstone of overcoming challenges. It's the ability to bounce back, to learn from setbacks and to keep moving forward. Cultivate a growth mindset, viewing challenges as opportunities for learning and development. Celebrate small victories, no matter how insignificant they may seem.

It's important to remember you are not alone in your struggles. Connect with other women who are facing similar challenges. Support networks can provide invaluable advice, encouragement and a sense of community.

Overcoming challenges is not about avoiding them, but about developing the tools and mindset to navigate them successfully. With determination, resilience and a supportive network, you can conquer any obstacle.

EMBRACING AUTHENTICITY

Authenticity is the cornerstone of a fulfilling life. It's about being true to yourself, embracing your flaws and living a life aligned with your values.

It's a journey of self-discovery, of shedding layers of societal conditioning to reveal the core of who you truly are.

Self-reflection is the first step. Spend time alone, journalling, meditating or simply observing your thoughts and feelings. What brings you joy? What are your passions? What are your values? Understanding your inner world is crucial to embracing your authenticity.

Vulnerability is often seen as a weakness, but really, it's a strength. Sharing your fears, doubts and imperfections creates genuine connections with others. It fosters empathy and understanding; you are not alone in your struggles.

Surround yourself with people who celebrate your authenticity. These are people who see you for who you are, flaws and all. They uplift and support you on your journey. Challenge societal norms and expectations. Don't be afraid to step outside of your comfort zone. Experiment with new things, explore different interests and discover your passions.

Authenticity is not a destination but a continuous journey. It requires courage, self-compassion and a willingness to be imperfect. Embrace the process, celebrate small victories and be kind to yourself.

As the poet Rumi said, 'The journey of a thousand miles begins with a single step.' Start by taking small steps towards authenticity. Over time, these steps will lead you to a life filled with purpose, passion and joy.

WOMEN LIVING FEARLESSLY

The journey from shadow to spotlight is a testament to the invincible spirit of women. It's a narrative of courage, resilience and the unwavering pursuit of authenticity.

From the confines of societal norms to the heights of personal liberation, we have traversed a path marked by both darkness and light. We have discovered the power within, the strength to break free and the courage to live fearlessly.

We have celebrated the strength found in vulnerability, the power of community and the joy of living authentically.

Remember, your story is unique, and your journey is yours alone. Embrace the twists and turns, the highs and lows. Every experience, every challenge, shapes you into the extraordinary person you are becoming. You are not a victim of circumstance, but a creator of your destiny. With courage, resilience and a belief in your own potential, you can overcome any obstacle. Let your light shine brightly, inspiring others to embark on their own journeys of self-discovery.

This book is an invitation to live fearlessly. It's a call to action to break free from the shackles of expectation and embrace the extraordinary woman you are. Remember, you are not alone. There is a sisterhood of courageous women cheering you on. Together, we can create a world where women are celebrated, empowered and living to their full potential.

So, step into the spotlight. Your story is waiting to be written. Live fearlessly!

Dr Patricia Gonde is the head of academics at Lusitania Primary School in Zimbabwe. She is an inspiring educator who has made a significant impact on the academic development of many students. Dr Gonde is also an international speaker and has participated in numerous webinars addressing important issues in today's educational landscape. She advocates for the modernisation of teaching methodologies and the integration of twenty-first-century skills into the curriculum to prepare students for the evolving workforce of the future.

In addition to her work in education, Dr Gonde is a prolific author, respected ambassador and researcher who has gained international recognition for her leadership and advocacy for quality education, gender equality and women's empowerment. Her dedication has earned her numerous prestigious awards, acknowledging her relentless efforts and social impact.

Dr Gonde delivers lectures to students from diverse countries and participates in conferences on the Sustainable Development Goals (SDGs). She also supports marginalised communities and aims to create entrepreneurial opportunities for women on a global scale. Dr Gonde has significantly contributed to education and women's empowerment in Zimbabwe. She has been involved in providing educational provisions for girls, donating library books and supporting orphanages to improve access to education and address basic needs. Additionally, under her leadership, the school has maintained a 100% pass rate for over a decade in grade seven results, and she has created opportunities for students to participate in global cultural exchange programs and attend national and

PATRICIA GONDE

international events. Dr Gonde has also founded the Heartfelt Teachers Network Globally and Girls Leading Our World to advance education and gender equality.

Dr Patricia Gonde's exemplary contributions to education and women's empowerment have been distinguished with several esteemed local and international awards, including the Global Educacio Eagle, Golden Globe and Africa Education Excellence awards. Her outstanding achievements in advocating for the SDGs further underscore her unwavering commitment to various social causes. Furthermore, Dr Gonde represented Zimbabwe as a diplomat at the Best Diplomats Dubai conference in 2024, where a diplomatic stance was drawn on the digital divide and its effect on SDG4, 8 and 9, demonstrating her multifaceted contributions as a global leader.

Her perseverance and leadership continue to serve as a beacon of hope and inspiration for educators and learners across the globe. Her transformative impact on education and women's empowerment resonates in Zimbabwe and globally, leaving an indelible mark on the world. Of notable recent mention, Dr Gonde received the esteemed gold award at the Woman Changing the World Awards in the category of Women in Education, presented by Dr Tererai Trent at Windsor Park in the UK. This distinguished event was graced by Sarah Ferguson, the Duchess of York, and brought together women awardees from around the globe, including Zimbabwe. She also received an award recently as one of Africa's one hundred most influential awards, an event held in Harare and organised by The Business Executive Group.

THE POWER OF UNLEARNING
FEAR OR DEAR

Pinar Sekmen

Secret, sacred and veiled ... We all have untold stories.

We all have encountered a time when we are compelled to rise from a fall, step on and walk through the broken pieces of our hearts, and propel ourselves into a state of mind in order to move on; to re-rise, re-shine and re-join the echo of our inner voices to resonate together as one. We may grow from these times and we may heal through these experiences, as long as we can manage to unlearn.

My experiential learning through my aha moments is what has shaped my path in my journey to self-discovery.

I believe it is high time I shared some of those mindful pieces of my peace, with my pure intention, which is not intended to preach, but echo your voice or at least accompany the reflection of your own journey of un/predicted, challenging or insecure times of turbulance through your unique storm.

'I don't know!'

Sometimes hard to say, sometimes an escape, sometimes embracing the truth, sometimes an innocent call for help and sometimes just a silence-filler. For me, it is my golden key to, and for, transformation; an invaluable heart and mind opener to my real 'me'.

> *'Seek the wisdom that will untie your knot. Seek the path that demands your whole being.'*
> **– Rumi**

I didn't know when I realised that 'I don't know' would be a magical touch on my immense awakening. It is now the simplest shortcut to defining *my* perception of wisdom in my awakening toward my inner journey that is still unfolding, non-stop, day by day, moment by moment. Yes, it is 'my' thought pattern; 'my' process of growth and 'my' wisdom. How could my personal experiences, my takeaways, my unique perception be generalised? As the nature of wisdom requires, its beauty and profoundness grow on a purposeful and long-lasting struggle to attain self-awareness. Whether attained or not, in the end, what matters would always be my reality in my realm of growth.

No one can or should dare to underestimate the power of empathy, as it is one of the codes set within human beings that not only conveys an eternal range of meaningful messages awaiting to be derived, but also takes us to deeper layers of understanding, even of the ones which have not been experienced personally. Willingness is the initiator to empathise with one another, to reach out to horizons. Isn't this what reshapes the whole approach, re-visions the core purpose of existence and rebuilds new, uncommon and unique perspecitves?

'What you seek is seeking you.'
– Rumi

My own experiential path, and the mutual fine touches upon each other's, has contributed to who I am today. I am a firm believer in the magical power of empathy. Otherwise, it would be unfair to take 'empathy' as only an ability of being in someone else's shoes, since this solely would never be sufficient to build a genuine bond or bridge between hearts and authentic stories. I remember the most common expressions uttered to me in my challenging times (but, to be honest, not the most healing) have been the words 'I understand you' or 'I feel you.' While I am deeply thankful for these sentiments, they coud only be meaningful with my own endeavours to dig into self-discovery. Some words could not go beyond positioning themselves as painkillers and could never create a holy halo in helping me overcome the situation or doing more to transform myself. This is a precious moment of enlightenment within a very crucial phase of healing in my treatment, maybe the first step to what I needed and sought. It was calling me to my own path of maturity.

> *'Don't feel lonely, the entire universe is inside you. Stop acting so small. You are the universe in ecstatic motion.'*
> *– Rumi*

That freezing cold in the surgery room…processing through the moments of self-doubt. Lying physically on the operation table, just as the flesh part of my whole being, with a hole in my being. I was constantly alert to jump over and not to be trapped therein. Looking up at the ceiling of emptiness with wet, blank eyes, surrounded by a crowd, but spiritually in a one-on-one session with my one and only power (with my core being). Witnessing so many gifted people with professional minds that had been sent to my service, ready to fix one of the overthinking swollen cables within my skull, and me, still trying arrogantly to arrange, control and organise the daily routines of my little daughters – as if no-one else would be able to care and handle all the mundane in life for them. With my little sincere prayers, hiding among vulnerable tears, impatient for the programmed numbness for me. Would it be better to disappear and get a bit lost in my subconsciousness for a couple of hours, or in my consciousness – maybe- forever? With a sprinkle of awareness, I might even leave that super(!) well-organised to-do-list behind. Was there really a possiblity of having other solutions or choices?

> *'The source of now is here.'*
> *– Rumi*

Apparently, it was.
Was it the traditional or cultural roots and the fixed mindset of

cowardness or laziness that prevented me from opening up and accepting the call to my freedom? Was it my ego that was capturing my mind and resisting the divine flow? Why would 'ego' be frustrated and hurt? And why would I worry about that? Had I been imprisoned within my ego all my life?

'Why do you stay in prison, when the door is so wide open?'
– Rumi

The moment I realised the essence and positivity of questioning for the sake of my personal growth and for the sake of seeking the means of healing to break the blurry mindset down into more simple patterns, was also the moment of shedding light on my self-realisation.

In the guidance of 'unlearning' and 'unknowing', I let my fears flow and find their own route for a new costume, or a mask, but, I knew that whatever would happen would be better for me and lead me to tap into my intuitive power in a re-shaped form.

'As you start to walk on the way, the way appears.'
– Rumi

The feeling of belonging to the right moment within the right mindset – whatever the conditions are – is priceless.

As my inspiration and motivation into seeking, priorly my self-awareness, for the sparks I needed to build in others has been my everlasting thirst, my last word will be again by Rumi, hoping to be an inspiration and an igniter:

'Yesterday I was clever so I tried to change the world. Today I am wise so I am changing myself.'
– Rumi

Today, I am deeply determined and ready to take the advantage of every blessing I have been granted, and to fill in at least a little gap within the rhythm and tone of my role in the relevant community of my moment to raise awareness and give voice to the unheard.

My unlearning allowed me to break free from the fears and constraints of established norms and practices.

Today, people think it takes financial power to reach professional growth. However, unless there is investment in personal growth through a profound level of introspection and self-awareness, it would only be a 'mission incomplete' in the the end, because of the beliefs they have held for a long time.

I heard my own scream to unlock my full potential to evolve and grow, to adapt to that 'being' I had been longing for. Unlearning encouraged, within me, a sense of agility by embracing curiosity and flexibility for a continuous growth.

It is true that the journey of unlearning requires courage as well. My comfort zone was there for me step outside of, and the fear of the unknown was calling me to be overcome. My unlearning helped me create my own space for new approaches as ingredients of my transformative experiences. Unlearning was something I liked and felt deeply in my veins, consciously this time. My knowledge needed to be updated, my experiences to be reflected, and my voice to be empowered for other silent voices. This shift not only enhanced my personal growth but also contributed to the platforms in continuous learning and improvement within organisations and communities. I found myself supporting educators, not only as a language mentor and coach, but also a holistic learning adviser in all terms. Unlearning is a vital process that requires agility, self-reflection, adaptability, courage and space for all these to gain a more fulfilling posture in life.

> 'The wound is the place where the light enters you.'
> – *Rumi*

The light entered me! In my uncertain traumatic times, but with my consent to open up to richer moments, to the more and to the beyond. Today, I love my wounds and the scars in my body and spirit. I honour the holes created through challenging times because that is what has enlightended me.

I intend to keep spreading the word of wisdom, the most powerful and educated form of building bond and empathy.

'Raise your words, not voice. It is rain that grows flowers, not thunder.'
*– **Rumi***

PINAR SEKMEN

Pinar Sekmen is a holistic learning advisor, a language coach and a teacher supporter (educator) who is based in Turkiye but has been working globally. She has been in the world of ELT (English language teaching) for over two decades. She has been trying to touch lives through her small business PS:Professional Support in Education. As an individual, a woman, an educator and a mother of two brilliant girls, she strongly believes in the power of holistic learning to grow in all aspects: mind, body and spirit. "Empathy" is her golden key and - rather than earned titles of 'ink'- for building bridges for an individual's personal and professional growth in that unique journey. Besides language education, she has been deeply interested in how to overcome the barriers encountered through a journey and how to set a goal for a meaningful outcome. She has also recently been working on trauma-sensitive teaching and learning environments and SEL (social emotional learning) focused studies on 'during and post-war and -earthquake' cases.

'... We all have untold stories: may be secret, sacred or veiled.

'We all have to step on and walk through the broken pieces of heart and mind to move on, re-rise and re-shine, and echo together as one. We grow on them ... we heal through them ... as long as we can manage to unlearn. And my experiential learning through my aha moments is what has shaped my path in my journey,' says Pinar.

As a lifelong learner, she has been working on taking advantage of every blessing she has been granted and filling in at least a little gap within the rhythm and tone of her role in the relevant community of the moment to raise awareness and voice the unheard.

THE JOURNEY TO BECOME

Ruvimbo Mazonde

Life is not always as easy as we might think and perceive. Life is full of ups and downs, but no matter the challenges and obstacles we might face, always rise up, dust yourself off and keep going until you reach your goal. My name is Ruvimbo Mazonde, and this is my story.

For as long as I can remember, I always had the feeling of *unbelonging* due to my experiences I encountered growing up. I grew up in a family of three and was raised by parents who were self-employed. They never had white-collar jobs and were considered *'the black sheep'* of the family. My father is a stonemason, and my mother is still a street vendor, making a living selling at a school gate in a high-density suburb, Mabvuku, in Harare, Zimbabwe. To the world, everything seemed okay, but all was not well. My mother was always in high spirits and jovial but behind the cheerful woman was hurt, pain and misery. My parents would fight regularly and had an estranged marriage; they were together but practically not together – it was more a marriage of convenience.

My father was not as successful as his sisters and the pressure was intense, especially with him being the only boy with five sisters. Everyone knows grandparents love their grandchildren, but for us it was not that simple with our grandmother. We were treated according to what our parents brought to the table. Due to the financial circumstances of my parents, we were raised in the family home. My parents have never owned their own home. I grew up sleeping on the floor with my sister in the dining room as the house only had two bedrooms and my brother was using the second bedroom.

Growing up at the family house was never easy, as it was one issue after another. At one point, the house was about to be sold without my father's knowledge, and he was told by a distant cousin what was going on. This caused many divisions, as only one of his sisters was against the house being sold. No-one cared where we would live. I still remember the family meetings as if it were yesterday. Not long after this, my father almost lost his life after he had eaten food containing smashed glass. All the blame was directed to my mother by his family. She was interrogated by the police, as she was the one who had prepared the food and was the prime suspect. We had all eaten the food, but glass was found only in his plate. This happened when we had an unexpected visitor at the time, and after a thorough investigation, Mum was exonerated and found innocent. The visitor (his brother) was found to be on the wrong side of the law, and surprisingly the charges were dropped, as they were going to deal with the matter as a family. However, they were prepared to take legal action against my mother but not his brother.

Despite everything going on with the family and my parents, I excelled academically and was the first person from my family to go to university. I graduated with an honours degree in psychology. Failure was never an option, as I knew the sacrifices being made for me to go through with university. In the rain, cold winds and scorching hot sun, my mother would be at the school gate by her table every single day selling snacks to school children. In as much as my mother never had the privilege to finish her primary school, she gave me the greatest gift of education. My parents had their own share of problems, but they were of one accord when it came to my education.

After graduating, I struggled to get a job in Zimbabwe due to the economy of the country. Instead of my father encouraging me and giving me hope, I was more of a burden to him. He would compare us to his nieces and nephews. Even though he would sometimes act irrational towards us, I still loved him as my father and will, always. I finally got a job at a law firm, and it was in the same year that I got married to a childhood friend, who I had met when I used to visit my aunt. I moved to South Africa to join him where he was working. I would be lying if I said it was easy; it was a bumpy road. There was a time when my husband was having issues at work and had to look for odd jobs, even if it meant cleaning people's houses to make ends meet. Through these difficult times, my mother would help me financially. As much as I was hurting that she needed to look after me, rather than me being the one to look after her, there was nothing I could do, I needed her financial support. I became pregnant and had many complications, spending a lot of time in hospital during my pregnancy. My mother was there throughout, and a strong support for me until I gave birth.

Years passed and things were not materialising in South Africa, but going back home to Zimbabwe was not an option either. We tried everything and anything to make ends meet and I was never ashamed, as my mother always told me to never be ashamed of anything as long as it brings food to the table. I had my own share of problems in my marriage, but it was nothing compared to what was to come.

Just after the pandemic in 2021, an opportunity came through for my husband to study in Poland. Instead of us celebrating, it ended up causing tensions. If something good comes your way after years of praying for an opportunity, you cannot explain the joy. However, I was made to look as if I was the enemy of progress by my husband's family, preventing him from succeeding in life. It's one thing to have people looking at you with a negative perspective and another to be reminded how poor your parents are, simply because an opportunity has been presented.

It was around this time we found out I was pregnant with our second child, and knowing the complications that came with my previous pregnancy, my husband decided he was not going to go for the March intake but would plan for the October intake instead. This did not sit well with my sister-in-law as she felt her brother was missing out on a big opportunity, because of me, but no-one knew the real reason behind his decision at that time. God works in mysterious ways, and it was during that same time that destiny helpers came through for me with the same opportunity; to go and study nursing in Poland, with my husband. This was the best news ever, but since I was expecting, we decided it was best for me to wait until after giving birth. I struggled health-wise and had a number of complications; this time around, it was even worse than my first pregnancy! I had a lung infection, severe pre-eclampsia, and other complications. In September 2021, I had an emergency C-section for the second time and almost lost my life, along with the baby. The both of us had to be placed in ICU.

Finally regaining my strength, I started working on my paperwork to go to Poland – all of this we kept between the two of us. During that time my marriage and faith were put to the test, due to negativity from my husband's family. The most difficult decision was to take my children back home to my mother, as I was preparing my paperwork to leave for Poland. They were too young to be away from their mother, but I had to take this bold step in order for them to have a brighter tomorrow. Again, this did not sit well with my husband's family, but my intuition was saying otherwise. I was surprised, but got my visa before my husband and we agreed we would leave together once he had his visa. We had arranged to spend some time with his family in Zimbabwe before our move to Poland. I then left South Africa a bit earlier to spend time with the children and my family.

He came to Zimbabwe a week later and I went to meet him on his arrival at the airport. The first encounter I had with my sister-in-law was chaotic. She had also gone to the airport to see her brother, and to take him home but she was shouting and throwing tantrums. I was confused but kept my cool. To say it was difficult living at my in-laws for those few weeks would be a huge understatement. My husband and I were arguing every day, and his family would stop every conversation the minute I walked into the room pertaining his trip to Poland. I had to ask for everything from his mother, since my husband was not working to assist me and I needed supplies for our children, including diapers.

The time came for my husband to leave and no-one said anything to me; I was to go directly to my own family. They didn't know it would be the last time they were going to see me for quite some time, as I was leaving for Poland myself two days later.

When I arrived in Poland, the fights in my marriage took a turn for the worst. His family were mad that I'd left without telling them, but I had left that decision up to my husband. Shortly after being in Poland, I fell ill, and it was one of the most difficult times of my life. It turned out I would need to see six different specialists, and it felt as if my life was falling apart. I started having suicidal thoughts. I wasn't going to give up on my boys, but my health kept deteriorating. I had no financial aid, and that meant I had to fend for myself, as well as trying to send money for my children back home. My tuition was paid for the first year only, so I had to pay for the remaining two years, as well as my upkeep and accommodation during the course of my study. I learnt to put all my faith and trust in the Lord and he surely came through for me. I got a job, and it was hard with my failing health, but I survived on painkillers to numb the pain.

I started loving myself and finding me again. I had to let go of all the anger, resentment, bitterness and hurt, and learn to forgive. I redirected all that energy into something positive, working with people and helping others around me. I didn't have much, but I would help where I could, with my own resources, and sometimes used my own situation as an example to strengthen others going through different challenges.

Even my marriage started improving despite everything, because I chose peace over justifying my cause. We embarked on mending our marriage and things have changed for the good. I even had to start working on my relations with my mother-in-law. I am not there yet, but I know I will get there eventually, as life is a journey.

I was nominated for The Women Changing the World Awards in

the Humanitarian Impact category and made it as a finalist; never did I think that those small gestures and deeds I was doing would have such an impact. I had raised the torch high for my family, as no-one ever thought such recognition would come my way. In my language there is a proverb that says *kukava datya kuriyambutsa* (to bite a lizard is to save it). If I had not been through what I went through, I would not have realised my full potential and be where I am today. Here I am, the first author in my family. God is indeed faithful; I get to share my story with the world. My faith has been renewed, my character and attitude has changed because now I know it does not matter your background, you can be anything you want to be in life, if you only believe in yourself. The following are some life lessons that were inspired by my challenges and serves as a reminder in my life:

- Life will test you, people will misunderstand you, but when criticism comes, do nothing, say nothing, as not everything requires you to react.
- Never ever look down on anybody no matter what unless you are admiring their shoes.
- We all make mistakes and wrong choices; but that should never hinder you from fulfilling your dreams.
- Always remember you can grow; without destroying others, you do not need to destroy others in order for you to grow we can all grow together.
- Finding satisfaction in the pain of others will never bring you true happiness, it takes so much energy for you to try to take other people's joy and happiness but you are not happy yourself.
- Become the good fire that genuinely lights up others, never take delight in causing another person pain.
- Never use your position of authority to inflict pain on others, life is uncertain and with no guarantees you never know what tomorrow has for you.

WOMEN LIVING FEARLESSLY

- We truly must genuinely love ourselves for who we are, surround yourself with people that appreciate you for who you are.
- Stop forcing yourself into spaces were people don't understand you; whether they are monied or not, extremely successful or not. Align yourself with people that value life through your perspective because you will lose your mind comparing yourself to people.

'In the middle of difficulty lies opportunity'.
– Albert Einstein

Challenges often bring growrh and new chances. Hard times change us – often for the better. I will forever be grateful to the Mukora family for realising the potential in me. You paved the way for me to do humanitarian work and help me advance academically. To someone going through challenges, I may not know the giant you are facing but not every situation is permanent. I have been rejected, mocked, misunderstood, hurt, lost friends, looked down upon but it took only one person to see the potential in me and invest in me, to change my life for the better. I fought through sicknesses and I'm still fighting financial struggles and marital problems; but here I am today, I am still going. We all can make the world a better place if we carry each other's burdens and love each other unconditionally. My family, husband and children are looking up to me and I cannot afford to disappoint them. I am determined to make my parents proud.

Ruvimbo Mazonde is a nursing student at WSEI University in Lublin Poland. She is now starting her third year of studies. She completed her BSc honours degree in psychology at Midlands State University in Zimbabwe in the year 2015.

She is an aspiring philanthropist and compassionate nursing student with a psychology edge: Bridging health care with empathy and understanding. Her work and career path are highly influenced by her background and life situations she has faced growing up to present. She is a devoted christian, wife, daughter and mother to two boys whom she loves dearly. She is a first-time author who had to share a glimpse of her life story with the world. When not immersed in her studies and humanitarian work, which she does on a smaller scale due to lack of funds, she enjoys cooking, watching movies, going out and spending time with her loved ones. She looks to inspire more people by her work and embark on philanthropy work on a larger scale as it has been her passion to give back to the community.

FROM DARKNESS TO EMPOWERMENT

MY FIGHT FOR JUSTICE

Sandra Spadanuda

In the depths of despair, I found myself engulfed by a darkness so profound that even the faintest glimmer of hope seemed but a distant memory. It was a place where the weight of depression, anxiety and relentless struggle bore down upon me with suffocating force, rendering every breath a Herculean effort. As I grappled with the overwhelming sense of defeat, I couldn't help but wonder how I had plummeted so far from the heights of my once highly esteemed career. The journey that led me to this point was paved with accolades and accomplishments, yet … it was precisely those successes that made me vulnerable to the cruel whims of fate. Then, like a thunderclap in the dead of night, the merciless glare of media scrutiny pierced through the darkness, casting my name and reputation into the unforgiving spotlight of public judgement. In an instant, everything I had worked tirelessly to build lay shattered at my feet, leaving me adrift in a sea of uncertainty and shame.

At the pinnacle of my career, I faced the unimaginable; I was arrested for a crime I did not commit. I was falsely accused of corruption.

I spent nearly three years fighting in court to clear my name, in a case that was ultimately dropped. When it was finally acknowledged that there was no case to answer, the decision seemed swift and effortless for them. Yet, for my family and me, it was anything but. There was no apology, no recognition of the immense pain and suffering we endured. We were pushed to the brink of bankruptcy, forced to refinance and repeatedly took out loans just to survive. In an instant, everything we had worked so hard for vanished.

Some might consider my arrest to have been unnecessarily excessive and heavy-handed. It took place during the busy morning rush at our family owned cafe, with customers present, while I was on long service leave. Six police officers – yes, six – were flown in from the nearest capital city, 1,500km away, to carry out this orchestrated and highly planned arrest, all based on the testimony of a single person. A testimony filled with untruths and lies, yet somehow, it was enough to trigger this drastic action.

A wrongful arrest is hard on anyone, but for us, as foster carers, the possibility of our boys being taken away was one of the scariest thoughts. It's chilling to think that someone's personal vendetta and hatred could risk the safety and wellbeing of our children. Purely for the chance to bring me down, they were willing to destroy our family.

In the end, the very person who initiated it all was the one whose statement was most inconsistent and flawed. Ironically, it was likely this flawed testimony was what led to the case being dropped. The state's star witness had lost credibility.

While I am grateful and blessed to be part of some incredibly supportive women's groups and movements, where we uplift and recognise each other, my daily life often lacks that same empowerment and support. Women have struggled enough against the patriarchy – why are we still fighting each other? We are powerful when we unite. Tearing each other down is not the answer. I believe deeply in the power of women supporting women.

Women have long been subjected to societal pressures and expectations that dictate how we should act, behave and talk. From a young age, many of us are taught to be polite, accommodating and agreeable, often at the expense of our own desires and opinions. These expectations often manifest in subtle ways – the pressure to smile, avoid confrontation, or prioritise others' comfort over our own. In more overt forms, women may feel compelled to conform to traditional roles or standards of beauty, even when these don't align with their authentic selves. The constant need to navigate these expectations can be exhausting and stifling, leaving us, as women, feeling trapped in a persona that doesn't reflect who we truly are.

WOMEN LIVING FEARLESSLY

These societal norms not only limit self-expression but also instill a deep-seated fear of judgement or rejection for stepping outside the prescribed boundaries. Breaking free from these pressures requires courage and a commitment to reclaiming one's voice, identity and agency – essential steps toward living a fearless and authentic life.

EMBRACING AUTHENTICITY

For years, I felt like I was living in a shadow – constantly trying to meet the expectations of others. Whether it was how I dressed, spoke or the choices I made, I often found myself sacrificing my own desires to fit into a mould that wasn't mine. The turning point came when I realised that no matter how much I tried to please others, I never felt fulfilled. It dawned on me that the only person who could truly define my worth and happiness was me. This realisation was both terrifying and liberating.

Letting go of others' expectations wasn't easy. It meant standing firm in my choices, even when they went against the grain. It required me to confront my fears head-on and be okay with not being liked by everyone. But with each step, I felt a sense of freedom I had never known before.

Living authentically has transformed my life in ways I never imagined. I now make decisions based on what feels right for me, rather than seeking approval from others. I've found that the more I embrace who I truly am, the more meaningful my connections become, and the more joy I experience. The fear that once held me back has been replaced by a deep sense of peace and confidence.

To every woman reading this, I want you to know that your journey is uniquely yours. Embrace it, honour it and don't be afraid to live on your own terms. When you choose authenticity over fear, you unlock a life of true fulfilment.

THE POWER OF SELF-WORTH

The power of self-worth is transformative. It allows you to live with confidence, resilience and authenticity. When you truly understand your value, you no longer feel the need to seek validation from others or compromise who you are. You become empowered to make choices that align with your true self, set boundaries that protect your wellbeing and face challenges with unwavering strength. Embracing your self-worth is a crucial step on the journey to living fearlessly - because when you know your worth, nothing can hold you back.

For years, I tied my sense of worth to external achievements and the opinions of others. But once I realised my worth wasn't dependent on these things, I experienced a profound shift. I began to see that my value was intrinsic, and it couldn't be diminished by anyone or anything. When you understand your self-worth, it changes the way you make decisions. You no longer feel the need to compromise your values or settle for less than you deserve. You start to make choices that reflect your true desires and honour your wellbeing, rather than trying to please others or fit into societal expectations.

Recognising my self-worth gave me the strength to say no to situations and people that didn't align with my values. I stopped compromising my happiness just to fit in or avoid conflict. This new-found clarity allowed me to pursue what truly mattered to me, without guilt or fear.

RESILIENCE THROUGH SELF-WORTH, BOUNDARIES AND EMPOWERMENT

Self-worth acts as a buffer against life's challenges. When you know your value, you're better equipped to handle setbacks, criticism and rejection. You're less likely to internalise negativity because you understand that these external events don't define who you are. This resilience is key to living fearlessly, as it allows you to move forward with confidence, even in the face of adversity. In the past, criticism would shake me to my core, making me question my abilities and my worth. But as I developed a stronger sense of self-worth, I became more resilient. I learned to take criticism in my stride, using it as a tool for growth rather than a measure of my value.

A strong sense of self-worth empowers you to set and maintain healthy boundaries. When you know your value, you no longer allow others to treat you in ways that are disrespectful or harmful. Setting boundaries becomes an act of self-care, reinforcing the message that you are worthy of respect and dignity. Understanding my self-worth helped me realise that it was okay to set boundaries – both in my personal and professional life. I no longer felt guilty for protecting my time, energy and peace of mind. Instead, I saw it as a necessary step in honouring my value.

Finally, I want to emphasise how self-worth leads to empowerment. When you recognise your worth, you stop looking for validation outside of yourself. You take ownership of your life and decisions, knowing you have the power to create the life you want. This sense of empowerment fuels your ability to live fearlessly and authentically. Realising my self-worth was a game-changer. It shifted my mindset from seeking validation to owning my power. I no longer waited for others to approve of my choices or tell me I was good enough. I knew my worth, and that gave me the confidence to pursue my dreams unapologetically.

EMERGING STRONGER

As I emerged from the darkest days of my ordeal, I began to see the world with new eyes. The pain and suffering I'd endured had given me a deeper appreciation for life's simple joys and a greater empathy for others' struggles. I found solace in nature, in the quiet moments of sunrise and the gentle rustling of leaves. These moments of peace became my refuge, a place where I could reconnect with myself and find the strength to keep moving forward.

With every challenge, my resolve grew stronger and my spirit more unyielding. I learned that resilience is not about avoiding pain but about embracing it, learning from it and using it as a catalyst for growth. The crucible of adversity had tempered my spirit, transforming me into a stronger, more compassionate and more determined individual.

My path to liberation has been neither straightforward nor easy. It has been a journey through the depths of despair, across the peaks of triumph and into the heart of my own being. It is a journey that continues to this day, one marked by an unwavering commitment to authenticity, resilience and self-discovery. I have learned that true liberation is not about escaping the trials of life but about embracing them, learning from them and allowing them to shape us into the people we are meant to be.

I have discovered the profound freedom that comes from living without fear, liberated from the weight of others' judgements. When faced with criticism or negativity, I understand that such remarks are more about the individuals making them than about me. Their opinions are a reflection of their own perspectives and issues, not a measure of my worth or character. I have learned to release myself from the burden of their perceptions, knowing that what others think, say or feel about me is ultimately none of my concern. By embracing this mindset, I am able to live authentically and fully, unshackled by external opinions and free to focus on my own path and purpose.

MOVING FORWARD AUTHENTICALLY AND FEARLESSLY

As we near the end of this chapter, I hope you find a renewed sense of inspiration and courage to live your life authentically. Embracing who you truly are, free from the constraints of others' expectations, is a profound act of self-empowerment. By shedding the weight of fear and judgement, you open yourself up to a life that is genuinely fulfilling and true to your own values and passions.

Remember, the journey towards living fearlessly is not always straightforward. It requires self-reflection, resilience and a willingness to confront and overcome the barriers imposed by external opinions. Yet, the rewards are immeasurable. When you choose to live authentically, you not only liberate yourself from the burden of others' perceptions but also pave the way for a more meaningful and purpose-driven existence.

As you move forward, let these insights guide you. Embrace your true self with confidence and know that the path to a fearless life is a continuous journey of growth and discovery. By doing so, you will not only transform your own life but also inspire those around you to break free from their own constraints and live authentically.

Here's to living fearlessly, and to the freedom and fulfilment that come with it.

PHOENIX IN THE SHADOWS

I fell where the world could no longer see,
In a pit carved from whispers and lies,
Wrongfully branded, shackled in shame,
I wandered through dark, endless skies.

Each bottle a lullaby to silence the storm,
Each tear a confession I never did speak,
As friends like ghosts faded away,
I drowned in the depths of the weak.

Loneliness carved its home in my bones,
The weight of injustice pressed on my chest,
But in the quiet of that bitter despair,
I found the courage to rise, to protest.

Through the fog of addiction, I fought for my name,
Each day a battle, each breath a spark,
From the ashes of blame and the ruin of me,
I built a new flame in the dark.

SANDRA SPADANUDA

Now I stand, not broken but reborn,
A warrior of truth in the face of the pain,
I carry my scars like banners of gold,
A phoenix who rose from the rain.

Now I walk with no chains to bind,
A woman unafraid of the fall,
I live with a fire that cannot be tamed,
Fearless, defiant, standing tall.

With every step, I own my past,
But it no longer owns me,
I rise with a heart that's fierce and free,
A woman who lives fearlessly.

A multi-award-winning foster carer, youth worker and service consultant, social entrepreneur, wellness advocate, international best-selling author, international speaker, fashion (runway and photographic) creative director and producer, and grooming and deportment educator, Sandra is described by many as a humble leader, change maker and social justice advocate. With a wealth of knowledge and experience spanning across the not-for-profit, local, state government and business Sectors, Sandra has worked in the youth, community and social services sector of Australia for over twenty-six years. She is employed as a public servant of the Western Australian state government, working full-time as a senior youth justice officer, while undertaking numerous other volunteer roles within her local community.

In 2015, Sandra co-founded Blue Beanie Projects, a registered health promotion charity aimed at reducing remote youth suicide rates and increasing regional and remote young people's access to professional, ethical and sustainable youth services. Blue Beanie work with young people to increase their social and emotional wellbeing, confidence, resilience, self-esteem and connection to community. Having lived and worked in some of Australia's most isolated and remote communities for most of her career, developing and implementing successful culturally appropriate youth service models, Sandra is particularly experienced and a passionate advocate for service needs of young people and youth workers in remote areas; and improving funding, training and resources for youth workers.

Sandra has faced significant adversity over recent years, enduring gruelling experiences following a wrongful arrest and criminal charges.

SANDRA SPADANUDA

After a three-year legal battle, during which state prosecutors ultimately applied to have her case formally dismissed, she emerged victorious. Sandra has since transformed from a victim to a hero, showcasing incredible resilience and serving as a role model, rewriting her narrative with courage and determination.

Driven by her own experience of a wrongful arrest, Sandra is a passionate advocate committed to raising awareness of the critical principle of 'innocent until proven guilty'. She seeks to educate the public on the importance of understanding that an arrest does not equate to guilt. Through her advocacy, she aims to shift the public mindset toward embracing this foundational legal principle.

Despite facing profound adversity and being wrongfully accused of a crime she did not commit, Sandra has demonstrated remarkable strength. Since this life-altering experience, she has co-authored and published three books, with two more slated for release this year. Her journey of overcoming such significant challenges and turning them into a platform for positive change is truly inspiring.

FROM BROKENNESS TO UNSTOPPABLE STRENGTH

RECLAIMING MY WORTH AND BUILDING A PREMIUM BRAND

Samantha J.

My journey from the depths of trauma to becoming Miss Australia 2025, a Woman Changing the World honouree and a seven-figure entrepreneur has been one of profound transformation. Rising from humble beginnings as a country farm girl in Wagga Wagga, NSW, I've faced unimaginable challenges, including sexual abuse, which shattered my sense of self-worth. However, through resilience, courage and an unwavering commitment to my healing, I rebuilt my identity and stepped into my power as a high-value CEO. Today, I proudly stand as a woman who has not only redefined her own life but also inspires other entrepreneurs changing the world to do the same.

THE BREAKING POINT: A SHATTERED SENSE OF SELF-WORTH

Growing up in Wagga Wagga, I was raised with a strong work ethic, shaped by my parents' relentless dedication to our family farm. My father, in particular, embodied the belief that success was directly proportional to hard work. This mentality became deeply ingrained in me from an early age, driving me to pursue success with a single-minded focus.

However, my world was turned upside-down when I became a victim of sexual abuse. The trauma was devastating, stripping me of my self-worth and leaving me feeling broken, worthless and undeserving. The shame and guilt I carried were suffocating, and for a long time, I buried the pain, believing that working harder and achieving more would somehow make me whole again.

At fourteen, I launched my first business, a clothing and jewellery accessory venture. On the surface, it appeared successful, but behind the scenes, I was struggling. I poured myself into my work, using it as a distraction from the unresolved trauma. The accolades I received and the early success of my business felt like a validation of my efforts, but deep down, I knew I was running from my pain.

The pressure to maintain this facade of success soon became overwhelming. I was driven by the desire to prove myself, to show the world that I was more than my trauma. But as I focused on proving my worth through external achievements, I neglected my wellbeing. I worked long hours, sacrificed sleep and isolated myself from friends and family. The thrill of entrepreneurship quickly turned into a cycle of exhaustion and self-doubt.

THE TURNING POINT: FACING THE PAIN AND RECLAIMING MY POWER

By the time I was nineteen, I had taken on the role of CEO of my family's property development company, Brunslea Park. Under my leadership, the business experienced extraordinary growth, expanding by 1,600% and reaching multi-eight figures. On the outside, it seemed like I had it all together, but the truth was far from it. The pressure to sustain this success was immense, and the unresolved trauma from my past continued to haunt me.

The breaking point came when I experienced burnout. The constant stress, coupled with the unresolved emotional pain, took a toll on my mental and physical health. I remember a particularly tough day when I felt completely overwhelmed, collapsing from exhaustion. It was a wake-up call that forced me to confront the trauma I had been running from.

I knew I couldn't continue down this path. The business model I had embraced – one that required relentless effort and sacrifice – was unsustainable. It was in this moment of crisis that I realised something had to change. I needed to heal, not just physically, but emotionally and spiritually. This realisation marked the beginning of my journey to reclaim my self-worth and rebuild my life and empire, from the inside out.

THE HEALING JOURNEY: EMBRACING VULNERABILITY AND SELF-COMPASSION

The path to healing was not easy. It required me to confront the pain I had buried for so long and to seek help. I travelled around the world, learning from the leading authorities in neuroscience, Shamanism, sacred sexuality, trauma and leadership, as I developed my unique methodology, The Illuminator Method, processing the trauma to rebuild my sense of self. Through this process, I learned that vulnerability was not a weakness but a strength. It allowed me to connect with my true self and to begin the journey of self-compassion and self-love.

During this time, I also launched Australia's first mental health webathon – Embrace4Bipolar. This project was deeply personal to me, as I had witnessed the impact of mental health issues within my own family. The webathon raised awareness and funds for mental health support, and it became a significant milestone in my career. It was through this work that I began to understand the importance of aligning my business with my values and using my platform to make a positive impact in the world.

As I continued to heal, I realised I needed to let go of the belief that self-worth was sourced externally, and instead had to become the source of my own self-worth. I began to redefine success on my terms, focusing on what truly mattered to me – living a life of purpose, integrity and impact. This shift in mindset was transformative, allowing me to step into my power as a high-value CEO and to build a business that was not only profitable, but also aligned with my values.

THE RISE: BUILDING A PREMIUM BRAND AND SCALING TO SEVEN FIGURES

With my new-found clarity and sense of self-worth, I began to reimagine my business. I realised that to achieve scalable success, I needed to embrace leverage and delegation. No longer could I do everything myself; I needed to build a team and create systems that supported my vision.

One of the most profound lessons I learned during this time was the power of leverage. By delegating responsibilities and trusting others with critical tasks, I was able to free myself from the day-to-day operations and focus on the aspects of my work I was truly passionate about. This shift allowed me to scale my business to seven figures while working just a few hours a day.

I also made the strategic decision to reposition my brand as a premium offering. This involved refining my services to focus on high-profit, high-impact areas that aligned with my values. I began working with personal brands, helping them scale to seven and eight figures with a focus on philanthropy and impact. This new direction reinvigorated my passion for my work and allowed me to make a more significant impact in the lives of others.

One of the most rewarding aspects of this journey has been the ability to empower others. Through my coaching and mentoring, I've helped entrepreneurs navigate their own challenges and build businesses that reflect their values and goals. One of my clients, an entrepreneur struggling with burnout, sought my guidance. Together, we restructured her business to align with her values and leverage her strengths. The transformation was remarkable – she experienced significant growth and rediscovered her passion for her work.

THE TRANSFORMATION: BECOMING A WOMAN CHANGING THE WORLD HONOUREE AND MISS AUSTRALIA 2025

As my business grew, so did my platform. I have since led thousands of illuminators – entrepreneurs who have turned their wounds and adversities into their greatest sources of wisdom, compassion and power, to build purposeful and profitable empires. Our next chapter started in 2024, when I opened the Illuminate Centre of Entrepreneurship Headquarters in Gold Coast, Australia. This centre represents the culmination of my journey, a place where entrepreneurs can come together to learn, grow and build businesses aligned with their values, with a vision to create one billion philanthropic impacts. The centre has quickly become a hub for innovation and collaboration, attracting leading minds in the industry. It symbolises my commitment to creating a positive impact and supporting the growth of others.

In 2023, I released my third solo bestselling book, *Illuminator*, which details my journey and the lessons I've learned along the way. The book has resonated with readers, inspiring them to take control of their lives and businesses. Additionally, I was honoured with the Top 40 Under 40 by Business Elites Award, recognising my contributions to the business community. These achievements are a testament to the impact of my journey and my commitment to helping others succeed.

But perhaps the most significant milestone in my journey was being honoured as a Woman Changing the World and being crowned Miss Australia 2025 for Miss Europe Continental. These accolades are not just a recognition of my achievements, but a celebration to the internal journey I have been through, to be an example to other women that our trauma does not define us, it's how we choose to respond that matters most, there are no limits on who we can be, other than self-imposed limits.

THE LEGACY: EMPOWERING OTHERS TO RECLAIM THEIR WORTH AND ACHIEVE THEIR POTENTIAL

My journey from brokenness to unstoppable strength has taught me that true success is not about external achievements, it's about reclaiming your worth, embracing your power and living a life aligned with the highest vision of your values that leads to long-lasting genuine fulfilment. Today, I am committed to using my platform to empower others to do the same.

SAMANTHA J.

I believe in growing our influence for impact, not vanity.

Through my mentoring, events and speaking engagements, I share my story and the lessons I've learned along the way. I help others navigate their own challenges, rebuild their self-worth and create businesses that are not only successful, but also deeply fulfilling. My mission is to inspire others to rise above their circumstances, to embrace their power and to make a positive impact in the world.

In reflecting on my journey, I encourage you to consider your own path. Whether you're facing trauma, burnout or simply seeking to make a greater impact, remember that you have the power to reclaim your worth and create the life and business you've always dreamed of. It's not about working harder – it's about working smarter, aligning your work with your values and embracing a sustainable approach to achieving your goals.

Focus on proximity. Proximity is power, and when you invest in a mentor who is where you want to be, you will soon be able to model their leadership, beliefs and behaviours, and fast-track the path towards your goals.

As I continue to grow and evolve, I am committed to staying true to my values and using my platform to create a legacy of impact. I believe we all have the potential to change the world, and it starts with reclaiming our worth, embracing our power and living a life of purpose and integrity.

FROM BROKENNESS TO EMPOWERMENT   A JOURNEY OF TRANSFORMATION

My story is one of transformation – from a young girl who felt broken and powerless to a woman who stands strong, empowered and ready to change the world. The journey has not been easy but it has been deeply rewarding. Through resilience, courage and a commitment to healing, I have reclaimed my worth and built a life and business that are aligned with my values.

Today, as Miss Australia 2025, a Woman Changing the World honouree and a seven-figure entrepreneur, I stand as a testament to the power of transformation. My journey is far from over, but I am proud of how far I've come. I am committed to continuing this journey, to empowering others and to creating a legacy of impact.

If there's one thing I've learned along the way it's that we all have the power to rise above our circumstances, to reclaim our worth and to create a life of purpose and fulfilment. My hope is that my story will inspire you to embrace your own power, to overcome your challenges and to live a life that reflects your true worth. Remember, you are not defined by your past – you are defined by the choices you make today and the life you create moving forward.

Samantha is an award-winning entrepreneur hailed as "The Illuminator" by Forbes for her trailblazing approach to purpose-led entrepreneurship. Turning her personal traumas into sources of hope, she created a multi-8-figure empire by the age of 22, overcoming challenges of sexual abuse and mental health.

A globetrotter and perpetual learner, Samantha has studied under leading experts in neuroscience, shamanism, sacred sexuality, trauma, entrepreneurship, and leadership. She developed her unique methodology, The Illuminator Method, to help entrepreneurs find deep fulfillment while building the life and 6-8+ figure empire of their dreams.

Recognized as one of Business Elite's Top 40 Under 40 entrepreneurs, Samantha is a 6x best-selling author and a 5x Women Changing the World award finalist and winner of the Women Changing The World - Emerging Leader of the Year (bronze).

She has been featured alongside Oprah, spent time with Richard Branson, the Duchess of York, and Dr. Terrai Trent. Her next book will be featured in the Oscars hampers and is being launched in New York in October 2024.

Samantha is representing Australia as Miss Australia 2025 in Italy at the Miss Europe International Continental. She has empowered thousands of entrepreneurs worldwide and is on a mission to make a billion philanthropic impacts through her business school and branding agency.

SURVIVAL MODE TO THRIVING MODE

Sara Knight

A brief glimpse into how I beat the statistics.

Who knew I would be here, writing about my life and the obstacles I had to overcome to achieve success? If you had asked me as a child, I would have told you I wanted to grow up to be a famous veterinarian, like Dr Harry Cooper or James Herriot. I would have said I wanted to travel the world and work with animals, and that all I desired was my mother's love and approval.

Unfortunately, fate had other plans and set me on a very different path. So here I am, writing about how I became a fearless woman and joined the other amazing, strong women to write this book.

I have survived a great deal in my thirty-nine years. I endured a turbulent childhood and survived two domestic violence relationships, where even today, they're still trying to affect me and my life.

I promise I won't let them.

One thing I have realised is that I'm not just a victim; *I am a strong female survivor*. This is the story of how I began the process to beat the odds and become an internationally award-winning photographer, business owner and speaker. Ultimately, this is the story of how I found my happiness, despite the drama and challenges around me.

I refuse to be defined by my circumstances – this is the part where you visualise Dory and the famous quote, *Just keep swimming*. I channelled my pain into my passion for photography, creating a space where I could express myself freely, to find solace in my art. My work began to gain recognition, and I soon found myself receiving international awards for my unique perspective and artistic vision as a female entrepreneur. Through my lens, I discovered a world where I was in control, where

I could capture beauty, even in the darkest of times. Beauty no-one thought to see.

Becoming a successful business owner and artist was a dream I had not dared to imagine during the darkest periods of my life. Yet, with each step forward, I proved to myself I was capable of more than I'd ever believed. Speaking at events and sharing my story with others became a source of empowerment, not only for me, but for those who heard about my journey.

Today, I stand proud as a testament to the strength of the human spirit. I am more than a survivor; I am a thriver. This is my story of resilience, triumph and the unyielding pursuit of happiness – how I found who I am meant to be and how I took the steps to this very moment. How I managed my C-PSTD, anxiety and ASD while kicking the world's backside.

So, what was my first step? Seeking proper mental health help was the first step towards my success.

As a child and young adult, I faced numerous challenges that left deep emotional scars. My turbulent childhood and subsequent abusive relationships took a toll on my mental wellbeing. I struggled with feelings of worthlessness, anxiety and depression. It was a dark period where the idea of seeking help seemed both daunting and futile.

The turning point came when I realised I could not navigate this journey alone. The weight of my past was too heavy to bear without professional guidance. Deciding to seek mental health support was a courageous step that marked the beginning of my healing process. I reached out to a therapist, uncertain of what to expect but hopeful for change.

Therapy provided a safe space for me to explore my emotions and experiences. It was through these sessions I began to understand the impact of my past on my present. My therapist helped me identify patterns of negative thinking and behaviour that were hindering my progress. This new-found awareness was instrumental in breaking the cycle of self-doubt and despair that had plagued me for so long.

One of the most significant benefits of therapy was learning coping mechanisms and strategies to manage my anxiety, depression and C-PTSD. At age twenty-eight, I was diagnosed with autism, something that helped me to change my life and better understand myself.

Under professional guidance, techniques such as mindfulness, cognitive-behavioural strategies and self-compassion exercises became essential tools in my mental health toolkit. These practices empowered me to take control of my thoughts and emotions, allowing me to respond to life's challenges with resilience and clarity.

The positive changes in my mental health had a profound impact on other aspects of my life. With a clearer mind and a stronger sense of self, I was able to pursue my passion for life with renewed vigour. My creativity flourished, leading to the establishment of my internationally award-winning business. The confidence I gained through therapy also enabled me to share my story and inspire others as a speaker and author.

Seeking proper mental health support was the foundational step towards my success. It allowed me to heal from the wounds of my past, develop resilience and embrace my potential. Therapy not only transformed my mental wellbeing but also paved the way for a fulfilling and successful life.

To this very day I still use the therapy tools I learned. They are essential in sustaining my wellbeing and continuing my journey of personal and professional growth.

The second step was to figure out what I wanted to do with my career. I took a year off to reflect and discuss my future with friends – and I had no idea my future husband was among these friends.

I have always had a love for photography since childhood, though I never considered it as a career option.

To me it was just a hobby, could I really make a career of it?

Through my conversations, I realised that my passion for capturing moments and telling stories through images could be more.

We are always happiest when we choose the things we love to do for a career.

In 2019, I decided to seriously pursue my passion for photography and enrolled in a certificate course in photography and digital imaging at my local community college. This decision marked a turning point in my life.

The experience was exhilarating!

Everything seemed to click into place. I made lasting friendships (shout out to my girl Hayley) and was guided by incredible mentors Adam Knott and Julian Watt who have years of experience and accolades in the photography world. Their support and encouragement were invaluable. Even today, they comment on how I was their most unique student, always eager to jump in feet first and embrace every opportunity. Something I will forever use to remind myself.

Did I have people put me down and tell me to give up? Yes!

Did I let them? No!

This journey not only honed my technical skills but also reinforced my confidence in my artistic vision, setting the stage for my career as an internationally recognised photographer. The choice to follow my passion has brought me immense joy and fulfilment.

I started with just a business name and a rented camera.

My third step was creating my business. I created a unique name that truly represented me and crafted a robust business plan with clear goals. I conducted extensive market research to understand my audience, while ensuring I remained true to my own moral and ethical beliefs.

One of my core principles is making professional photography accessible to all.

I take great pride in my ability to budget effectively, allowing me to offer low-cost, high-quality photos to families who might otherwise struggle to afford them. Everyone deserves to have beautiful, happy memories captured and preserved. One of my business codes is 'no discrimination' – I do not turn anyone away.

Building this business was more than just a professional endeavour, it was a deeply personal mission. I wanted to create something that reflected my values and passions.

From brainstorming the perfect name to setting realistic and ambitious goals, every step was a labour of love – and staying true to my ethical standards was crucial. It guided my decisions and helped me carve out a niche in the market that resonated with clients who shared similar values. This approach not only distinguished my business but also brought immense pride and satisfaction, knowing I was providing a valuable service to the community. My business became a testament to my dedication, to both my craft and my principles.

My belief is true success is not measured by how much money you earn but by the appreciation and value others place on your work.

It is the genuine connections and the impact you make that define real achievement. When people truly value what you do, it signifies that your efforts and passion resonate with them. This acknowledgement and respect from others provide a profound sense of fulfilment.

My success, therefore, is found in the meaningful relationships and lasting impressions I create through my dedication and artistry, rather than merely in financial gain.

My business has been operating for five years now which leads to my next and final step … well at least for this chapter.

Don't let anything stop you from jumping in feet first!

It takes great bravery to step out of your comfort zone, to find the courage, to speak up and throw yourself into the fray. It's not about knowing every outcome or having a perfect plan, it's about the audacity to embrace the unknown, to push boundaries and to transform challenges into stepping stones. Each leap is a testament to my commitment to living fully, learning and evolving. By jumping in feet first, I turn every fear into a catalyst for courage, forging a path where the only limit is my own willingness to leap again.

My advice to anyone reading this is simple – bite the bullet. Embrace every opportunity and put yourself out there. One significant step I took was joining my local Chamber of Commerce here in Penrith, NSW. Initially, meeting new people felt nerve-wracking, but I'm so glad I pushed through.

From this experience, I gained invaluable connections, including a mentor, Mr Fox, whose guidance has been instrumental. I've built a network that feels like a family, surrounded by local businesspeople who offer support and insight. This move opened doors to new opportunities and provided a solid foundation for my business.

Taking that leap was intimidating, but it transformed my professional life in ways I hadn't anticipated. The connections and advice I received have been crucial to my growth and success. So, don't shy away from stepping out of your comfort zone. Dive in with courage, and you'll find that the rewards often outweigh the initial discomfort. Each challenge you face is a chance to build something meaningful and to grow beyond what you thought possible.

Additionally, don't overlook the value of entering awards. Submitting applications and competing in these events can be daunting, but winning has been a game changer for me. It's not just about the recognition, it's about validating your efforts and gaining credibility.

Winning awards has boosted my confidence and brought my work to a broader audience. Each accolade is a testament to stepping out of my comfort zone and pursuing excellence with determination. So again, dive in with courage, and you'll find the rewards often outweigh the initial discomfort.

This journey has also led me to meeting and collaborating with the incredible women of the AusMumpreneur team. Meeting these driven, inspiring entrepreneurs has been transformative. Their support and camaraderie have enriched my business journey and, personally, have boosted my confidence.

Finding happiness was perhaps the greatest triumph of all. It did not come from the approval of others or from achieving fame. Instead, it came from within, from acknowledging my worth, embracing my journey and celebrating my survival. Despite the lingering shadows of my past, I have built a life filled with joy, creativity and purpose.

In my final thoughts:

I learned that external validation is fleeting. The recognition and happiness, I discovered, is an inside job. It required me to look inward, to confront the painful memories of my past and to reconcile with the person I had become. It was not an easy path. The journey towards self-acceptance and inner peace demanded courage, resilience and an unwavering commitment to personal growth.

The shadows of my past, marked by domestic and family violence, often threatened to overshadow my progress. These experiences, while harrowing, became the crucibles in which my strength and determination were forged. I refused to let these dark chapters define me. Instead, I chose to see them as integral parts of my story; chapters that contributed to my resilience and depth of character. By acknowledging and embracing these experiences, I was able to transform my pain into a source of profound strength and inspiration.

Creativity became my sanctuary and my expression of liberation. Through my lens as a photographer, I found a way to channel my emotions and tell my story. Each photograph became a testament to my journey, a visual narrative that captured the essence of my resilience and hope. The process of creating art allowed me to process my emotions, heal and, ultimately, thrive. It provided a sense of purpose and fulfilment that transcended accolades and recognition.

Building a life filled with joy required me to cultivate a mindset of gratitude and mindfulness. I learned to appreciate the small moments of beauty and connection in everyday life. Whether it was the warmth of the morning sun, the laughter of a friend or the satisfaction of being a creative émigré, I found joy in the present moment. Mindfulness taught me to be fully present, to savour the experiences and to find peace in the here and now.

My journey towards fulfilment was also deeply intertwined with my commitment to helping others. By sharing my story and advocating for survivors of domestic and family violence, I found a profound sense of purpose. Each person I reached, each life I touched, reinforced my belief that my experiences, though painful, had a greater meaning. They became a source of hope and encouragement for others walking a similar path.

In essence, finding happiness was not about escaping my past but rather integrating it into a life of meaning and purpose. It was about celebrating my survival and recognising that every experience, every challenge, had shaped me into the person I am today. Happiness, I realised, is a state of being that comes from within, a reflection of self-love, acceptance and the unwavering belief in one's own worth. As I continue to walk this path, I carry with me the lessons of my journey, knowing that true happiness is the greatest triumph of all.

There is a quote spoken by Robin Williams in the movie, *Dead Poet's Society* by Tom Schulman, that inspired my life: *'No matter what people tell you, words and ideas can change the world.'* All you have to do is try – only you stand in the way of your path.

Sara Louise is a thirty-nine-year-old accomplished photographer and mum to six. She is the creative force behind Sara Louise Photography, a thriving business known for its captivating and evocative images. Based in Australia, Sara's journey in photography has been marked by both personal triumphs and professional accolades, reflecting her resilience, talent and unyielding passion for the art form.

As an individual with autism with C-PTSD and a survivor of domestic and family violence, she found solace and expression through the lens of her camera. Photography became a powerful medium for her to communicate her unique perspective and experiences, allowing her to connect with others in profound ways. This personal connection to her work is evident in the emotive quality of her photographs, which resonate with viewers around the world.

In the last two years, Sara Louise Photography has experienced remarkable success. Sara was honoured with the prestigious title of International Street Photographer of the Year 2022/2023/2024, a testament to her skill and vision in capturing the raw beauty of everyday life. Her work has garnered widespread recognition, earning her nominations for several significant awards, including the BX Awards, Women's Championship, Australian Ladies in Business and Mono Awards and winning others like local business awards 2002. These accolades highlight not only her technical proficiency but also her ability to tell compelling stories through her images.

Sara's photography is characterised by a keen eye for detail, a deep understanding of light and shadow and an innate ability to capture fleeting moments of emotion and connection. Her portfolio is diverse, ranging from striking street photography to intimate portraits and evocative landscapes. Each photograph is a testament to her dedication to the craft and her unwavering commitment to producing work of the highest quality.

Beyond her professional achievements, Sara is also a passionate advocate for mental health awareness and domestic violence survivors. She uses her platform to raise awareness and inspire others, sharing her story to empower those who may be facing similar challenges. Her advocacy work is an integral part of her mission, underscoring her belief in the transformative power of art and storytelling and another reason to share who she is by authoring or co-authoring in books.

Sara Louise Photography has not only become a recognised name in the industry but also a symbol of resilience and hope. With a growing clientele and a portfolio that continues to expand, Sara's future in photography looks incredibly bright. Her journey is a testament to the strength of the human spirit and the power of art to heal, inspire and connect us all.

RISING FROM THE ASHES

A PHOENIX IN THE MAKING

Sarah MacRae

INTRODUCTION: THE FLAMES OF BETRAYAL

Life is a journey paved with both joy and pain, growth and loss. We encounter people who change our lives for the better, and, at times, for the worse. My story begins with a deep betrayal from someone I once considered family – a person I trusted implicitly, who shattered my world in a way I never imagined. But this chapter isn't just about betrayal. It's about what came after – the rebirth, the rise from the ashes and the creation of a new, even bigger dream. This is the story of how I found the meaning of the phoenix and became one myself.

THE BETRAYAL: A SHATTERING BLOW

The initial sting of betrayal is something that's hard to put into words. It's a deep and searing pain that leaves you gasping for air. When it comes from someone you trust, it's even more devastating.

For years, I nurtured a close relationship with this person – let's call them 'Alex' – who felt like a sibling. Our bond was as strong as any familial tie, filled with shared dreams, secrets and a mutual understanding of each other's lives. We supported one another through thick and thin, and I never once doubted Alex's loyalty.

But life has a way of unveiling the truth when you least expect it. After losing my mentor a few years prior to cancer – a person with whom I had built this legacy – life had already dealt me a heavy blow. We had faced countless challenges together, and I had made a promise to her that I would always be there for her daughter, who was like a sister to me. But when betrayal came from her daughter, it wasn't just a personal loss; it was a complete destruction of a long-standing family bond and the legacy we had worked so hard to create. Money and greed had become more important than the history, love and dreams we had nurtured together.

This betrayal wasn't just about breaking trust; it was a full-scale dismantling of everything I thought I knew. Alex's actions were premeditated, cold and calculated. I was left in the ruins of our relationship, questioning everything I believed in.

THE AFTERMATH: NAVIGATING THE DARKNESS

After the betrayal, I entered a dark period – a time of grief, confusion and intense pain. It felt as though the world I knew had crumbled, leaving me to pick up the pieces alone.

During this time, I wrestled with anger, sorrow and a deep sense of loss. I questioned my own judgement – *How could I have been so blind? How could I not have seen the signs?* My self-esteem took a hit, and for a while, I lost sight of who I was and what I stood for.

It was in this darkness that the concept of the phoenix first entered my mind. The phoenix, a mythical bird that rises from its ashes, seemed to mirror my own need for rebirth. But at that time, I felt anything but powerful. I was broken, defeated and unsure of how to move forward. The idea of rising again seemed impossible. I was alone, in the dark, struggling to find a flicker of light.

THE TURNING POINT: DISCOVERING THE PHOENIX WITHIN

Grief has a way of changing you. During my sorrow, I found myself reflecting on the story of the phoenix more and more. The phoenix, after all, is not just a symbol of rebirth, but of transformation through fire. It undergoes immense pain and destruction, only to emerge stronger and more magnificent than before.

I began to see my betrayal and loss as my own 'fire'. It was an all-consuming blaze that had the potential to destroy me, but also the power to forge something new. Slowly, I started to understand I had a choice. I could let the flames consume me entirely, or I could rise from them, reborn. The phoenix was no longer just a distant myth; it became a symbol of what I could become; a force of nature, resilient and unyielding.

This realisation didn't come all at once. It was gradual, like dawn breaking after a long night. I started to gather the pieces of my shattered self, examining them one by one. *Who was I? What did I want?* And more importantly, *who did I want to become?*

THE RISE: BUILDING A NEW DREAM

As I began to heal, I realised that the dream I had lost wasn't the end. It was a chapter in a much larger story – my story. The fire of betrayal and loss had cleared the way for something new, something even greater than I had previously imagined. I decided that it was time to dream again, but this time, my dream would be bigger, bolder and entirely my own.

Creating a new dream wasn't easy. It required introspection, courage and a willingness to step into the unknown. I had to let go of the old dreams, the ones tied to my mentor and to Alex, and allow myself to envision a future that was entirely my own.

I began to ask myself, *What do I truly want?* The answer wasn't immediate, but it began to take shape over time. I wanted to help others find their strength, especially those living with disabilities and mental health challenges, to empower them to rise from their own ashes. I wanted to build something that could inspire others to overcome their darkest moments and emerge stronger, just as I had.

And so, the seeds of my new dream were planted. I envisioned a platform – a community where people could come together to share their stories, support one another and find their own inner phoenix. This wasn't just about me anymore; it was about creating a movement of fearless people, rising together from the ashes of their pasts.

SARAH MACRAE

THE REBIRTH: CRAFTING THE VISION

The process of crafting this vision was both challenging and exhilarating. I had to confront my fears, doubts and insecurities head-on. But each step forward was a step away from the pain of betrayal and a step closer to something beautiful.

I started rebuilding my dream to support people living with disabilities and mental health challenges, who had been lost in the system or were just too complex. My new dream team began to form, made up of people with both the right and wrong intentions. But I had become aware of hidden agendas and had learned through the loss of loved ones to see people for who they truly were. Our new tribe formed quickly, as if the universe had aligned us together. These people had all been through their own fires, and their stories resonated deeply with me. I realised that I wasn't alone; there were so many of us who had been through the flames and had the potential to rise again.

With their support, I began to build the foundation of my new dream. I created a platform where people could share their stories, find resources for healing and connect with others who understood their journey. This platform wasn't just a place of business or a service, it was a safe haven, a place where people could find solace and strength.

I called it 'Phoenix Rising' – a name that encapsulated everything I had been through and everything I wanted this community to represent. It was about transformation, resilience and the power of rebirth. Phoenix Rising became my new dream, a dream that was not just about me, but about all of us who had been through the fire and emerged stronger.

THE TRIBE: CREATING A COMMUNITY OF PHOENIXES

As Phoenix Rising grew, it became more than just a platform – it became a tribe, a community of people who understood what it meant to rise from the ashes. This tribe wasn't just a collection of individuals; it was a community bound by shared experiences and a collective strength.

The people in this tribe supported one another in ways that were truly remarkable. They shared their stories, offered advice and provided a shoulder to lean on during tough times. The connections formed within Phoenix Rising were deep and meaningful, built on the foundation of trust and mutual respect.

Together, we created a space where vulnerability was met with compassion, where struggles were met with understanding and where triumphs were celebrated with genuine joy. This tribe became a home away from home for many – a place where they could be themselves, without fear of judgement.

In this safe haven, we found the strength to confront our pasts, to heal our wounds and to build new dreams. The tribe wasn't just about surviving, it was about thriving, about using our experiences to grow and to empower one another. It was a living, breathing embodiment of the phoenix; constantly rising, constantly evolving.

THE ACTIVITY HUB: REBUILDING MY VISION

RISING FROM THE ASHES: A PHOENIX IN THE MAKING

This space became a beacon of hope, a place where our community could escape the challenges of the outside world and focus on their own growth. It was a refuge, a sanctuary, a place where they could find the strength to rise again.

REBUILDING MY NAME AND REPUTATION: A JOURNEY OF RESILIENCE

As I worked on creating this hub and growing our tribe, I also faced the challenge of rebuilding my name and reputation. The betrayal I had experienced had left its mark, and I knew that in order to move forward, I had to reclaim my identity and rebuild the trust I had lost, not just with others, but with myself.

The journey to restore my reputation was not easy. It required a steadfast commitment to my new vision and a refusal to be defined by the actions of those who had wronged me. I understood that rebuilding trust would take time and consistency. Every decision I made, every step I took, was an opportunity to demonstrate who I truly was; a person of integrity, resilience and unwavering dedication to my mission.

I began by being transparent about my experiences, sharing my story of betrayal and rebirth with those who mattered. I found that honesty, even when painful, was the key to healing and restoring my reputation. I made it a point to lead by example, showing through my actions that I was committed to the values of Phoenix Rising: authenticity, compassion and empowerment.

I also focused on the quality of the work we were doing at the hub. By creating meaningful programs and providing genuine support to our community, I was able to prove that Phoenix Rising was not just a dream, it was a living, breathing reality making a real difference in people's lives. The success of the hub became a testament to my resilience and a symbol of the new path I had chosen.

Gradually, as the hub flourished and our tribe grew stronger, the shadow of betrayal began to fade. My name became associated not with the pain of the past, but with the hope and strength of the future. People began to see me not as a victim, but as a phoenix, a symbol of transformation and rebirth.

A NEW DAWN: EMBRACING THE FUTURE

As I stand on the other side of this journey, I realise the betrayal that once threatened to destroy me has, in fact, been the catalyst for the most profound transformation of my life. The fire that consumed my old dreams has forged a new, stronger and more resilient version of myself. I am no longer defined by what was taken from me, but by what I have created in its place.

Phoenix Rising is more than just a hub or a community; it is the embodiment of a new beginning – a place where people who have faced their own fires can come together, find support and rise again. It is a testament to the power of resilience, the strength of community and the beauty of transformation.

Looking ahead, I am filled with a sense of purpose and optimism. I know there will always be challenges, but I also know I have the strength to face them. My journey has taught me that from the deepest pain can come the greatest growth, and that every ending is also a beginning.

The phoenix within me continues to rise, and with it, so does Phoenix Rising. Together with my tribe, we will continue to build, to grow and to inspire others to find their own strength, their own resilience and their own ability to rise from the ashes. This is just the beginning of our story; a story of hope, of healing and of the unbreakable human spirit.

Hi, I would like to introduce myself. My name is Sarah MacRae, the eldest of four siblings, born and raised amidst the picturesque freezing landscapes of the Southern Highlands. My journey has been one of resilience and transformation, despite facing personal tragedy, such as the loss of my youngest brother, Keith. Throughout these challenges, I've achieved milestones that I am genuinely honoured to share.

I'm a proud mother to two amazing girls, Emily-May and Macie, who are the centre of my universe. My greatest achievements are undoubtedly my children, and I am deeply grateful for the unwavering love and support from my incredible partner, Rael. Rekindling our high school romance twenty-five years later, Rael has been my soulmate and my strength. My family and close-knit tribe mean everything to me, especially my youngest daughter, who, at just eight years old, faces challenges with ASD and complex trauma. Her resilience is awe-inspiring and motivates me to keep going through life's ups and downs.

Balancing motherhood and running my own business isn't easy, but it's a challenge I embrace with grace and courage. My dedication to my daughters' wellbeing drives me forward, pushing me to overcome obstacles and seize every moment.

With twenty-seven years of experience in the disability field, advocacy is in my blood. It's a privilege to speak up for those who often don't have a voice of their own. I am on a mission to raise awareness and promote inclusivity. Everyone deserves to be valued and empowered, regardless of their abilities.

I have a relentless drive that stems from transforming my emotions of anger and hurt into a powerful force for creating and achieving societal change or nurturing my daughters' growth, I give it my all. Each day is an opportunity to make a positive impact.

In my story, you'll find a blend of resilience, compassion and determination. I'm here to leave my mark, to inspire others to embrace their journey and to make a difference in the world. With every step I take, I'm reminded that the greatest achievements often come from the toughest challenges.

Beyond my roles as a mother and advocate, I've had the privilege of being involved in various community initiatives. Giving back to the community is a core value I hold dear. I've seen firsthand the power of collective action and its positive impact on the world around us.

Looking ahead, I'm excited to continue my journey of growth and impact. Whether expanding, growing my business or simply being there for my family, I'm committed to making the most of every opportunity. As I navigate the road ahead, I'm grateful for the love and support of those who have been by my side every step of the way.

With love in my heart and fire in my soul, I'm ready to take on whatever challenges lie ahead continuing making a positive impact in the lives of others.

Website: 247careservices.com.au
Email: sarah@247careservices.com.au

EVEN
Sofía Calvo Niño

I close my eyes when the sun yields its place to the embrace of the night. However, the moon is born to guide in his presence. I cross the core of memory to search for the eternal light that illuminates words. An electrifying feeling is my only companion. The pulse of my heart accelerates and stumbles, to stop short at times due to the memories imprisoned in its centre. Memory still sharp; intense in its heart, living memory.

Tears fall from my eyes and soak up the words engendered in my soul. The cry of pain of the spirit that cries out resonates in my head:

How can human beings suffer colossal impacts without failing in the attempt not to lose their last breath?

A whirlwind of thoughts soaks deep like rain. I pray:

God, I have felt your constant protection throughout my path through this valley of tears, I have slept with the comfort of a new dawn. Please don't let me go!

My body collapses face down to the ground, crying without consolation.

Breathe, Sofi! Don't you see the beautiful sun rising behind the hill? It is a memory that bleeds but I'll take care of you and carry you in my arms because you know the path, that same path that one day, you yourself also travelled.

I feel compassion and love bloom in my soul towards the unfortunate, as the scorching wind ravages my body.

I choose to extend my hands to help those who breathe adversity and embrace them in their misfortune. I declare inwardly while the warm sun caresses my cheeks, as I take steps along the already known path.

A repetitive thought, like a spell, brings me back to myself.

SOFIA CALVO NIÑO

Prepare to live, not to die, although life is so fragile, because we are souls inhabiting a body.

I smile as I hug the children after stroking their hair, but I hear one crying uncontrollably. I stop my feet for a moment, confused between the passageways of the orphanage. I can't find the child who needs me, and I burst into tears. And then a hand touches my shoulder, and a voice calms my anguish:

Sofi, wake up! It's just a nightmare. My husband's warm gaze consoles the torment of what I experienced eight years ago, relived in the dream of that distant night.

I continue my way towards the building with eyes full of tears. Skies of hope clouded by clouds of despair pass, through the fragile glass. I am confused with the people running frantically inside. I push the door where my feet take me and there, with oxygen hanging from a bag, surrounded by the heroes in white coats, he lies. He, whom I loved to the fullest extent of his being and whose hands dried countless times the tears flooding my skin.

I don't remember the fainting or how long it lasted. In my opinion, it was just a few seconds, although according to the nurse, who attended me in another white cubicle, it was more than four hours. I go back and the date on the calendar marks almost seven months in which my back-and-forth in the clinic has known no rest. I re-enter the room to immerse myself in the loving eyes of my begging husband:

Darling, go back to our home. You can't stay here with me, you need to rest.

What home? – I ask – *The empty house with cold walls? Home is here with you, because you are my home!*

Live love to the fullest, it is a joy to find someone who loves us with deep love, respect and gratitude. Every day shared will be a gift.

WOMEN LIVING FEARLESSLY

SUNSET

The weeks seemed like deep red autumn leaves falling to the ground with no hope of returning to a blossoming spring.

The days advanced, among nurses and patients, in white labyrinths of cold passages. My violin accompanied me. I longed for the melody of his voice flooding the rooms to be a ray of light that cheered the souls of those who already saw the final line of the marathon called 'life'.

One day in the morning of that October 2016, after playing my husband a beautiful melody, he stated with a courageous voice:

Darling, please, be strong. I will go to the house of the heavenly father. I'll wait for you there.

I vaguely remember how time stopped, although I doubt the precise moment of the statement in which life took a 180° turn. I was unable to utter any words, only the muteness of my broken soul seemed to take palpable form. That autumn was dyed black after losing, in the unequal fight against terminal cancer, the most wonderful man that God could give me in life.

When we are born they prepare us to live, but not to face death. Live consciously because no-one will live for you. Love, smile and be happy.

CLOSED NIGHT

The twilight was increasingly dense, the darkness weaving the central verses of the lullabies of death. Just a few days after taking my beloved, the Grim Reaper became infatuated with the fruit she carried in my womb and that was all that was left of my deceased husband to love, in my lap and in my arms. The scythe stabbed into me with such force that it made me writhe in intense pain. The ambulance came in a few minutes to take me to the emergency room.

We must save the baby! was the mantra repeated in my head, that also took over the mouths of the health workers who treated me.

'We need oxygen! ... We're losing her! ...' ...

...   ...

'The doctor will come to talk to you,' the nurse assured, behind whose body the wooden crucifix emerged, nailed to the skin of that white wall. And that was when I knew it, long before the doctor's painful statement:

'You need to be strong, the baby is in God's arms.'

I felt death not only in my gut. It climbed and descended over my entire body, reducing me to a lonely, empty shadow.

They both left! she repeated incredulously.

Time ceased to exist, the nights merged with the days, the memories flooded my soul that cried inconsolably many times.

Cry, my soul, cry without consolation, cry because I need to hear your tears fall.

Cry, my soul, cry without consolation, for when I hear you cry, my belly cries.

We are spiritual beings breathing from within corporeal matter. Children are of life. And even though we face trials, God always has a plan in every life so that we rest in peace, love and compassion.

NO MOON

The deadly triad would deliver the final blow a few hours from the Peruvian capital, carrying my mother's name, written on the cold steel of its hungry scythe.

Many autumns and winters had knocked on my door, while I still lived in that house full of memories of life-giving happiness.

We must be grateful for what we enjoyed and for what is still in our lives.

LIGHT CLEARANCE

The odyssey of my living hell took me to the doors of the Lord.

Where are you, oh God? Anguish accompanies me, pain eats away at my bones, misfortune has taken hold of me. I walk in the shadows, my wings are broken. I have no consolation.

The months passed, the seasons of the year took their course, the pain sank me into a huge muddy swamp.

I can't take it any more, I'm drowning! I sobbed.

Within my anguish and despair a voice called me. I felt a hand rubbing mine to help me out. I couldn't see, but I felt his presence and an enormous peace invaded my being.

God, is it you?

Why is there so much pain and affliction in my life?

Please stay with me because I'm afraid and filled with anguish and pain.

And I heard:

God prepares his best soldiers for special missions.

Trust in God's will, faith is an anchor that keeps us firm.

TWILIGHT

Days turned into months, and months turned into years.

One winter night, I decided to visit the hospital for cancer patients, at a time when the noise was dying down and the visitors had already left. There I was confronted with a harrowing reality. The corridors and gardens of the hospital reminded me of a human swarm. However, in this hive, the sick slept covered by cardboard and newspapers in a vain attempt to shelter from the relentless cold in the city of Lima. Sick people who had come from the interior of the country waiting for appointments to be seen.

Oh God! It still hurts to return to this image, mothers with small children hanging from their arms and elderly people shivering under the harshness of the inclement weather.

The sobs of a child transported me back to the past. My desperation led me to follow the sound of his crying. How much pain my soul harbours! So much so that it tore me apart inside. Behind some bushes I managed to find the child. I hugged him to protect him and took off my coat, covering his tiny body with it and began to rock him with the lullaby that my grandfather sang to me when I was a child.

> *'Let my child fall asleep, let my sun fall asleep*
> *Go to sleep, my heart.'*

What has become of him and his mother? I still wonder.

That night I returned home exhausted. I slept little and with constant shocks, but I had a clear understanding that my path was, definitely, to walk alongside those in need.

The days took their course and the weeks their hours. Between the comings and goings of orphanages and the hospital for cancer patients, the months slipped by, and the years accumulated.

Spring has arrived. One morning, while I was enjoying my cup of coffee, I was contemplating, through the window, the beautiful hummingbird that fluttered near the gerberas, my favourite flowers, the flowers I planted with much love and that gave me the scent of their petals as they bloomed. It was then that I received an unexpected call that would mark another turning point. Sister Gloria, a Mercedarian nun, was calling. *What a joy!* I answered immediately. We chatted for a while when she asked me to visit her. How could I not please her, she was the best religion teacher I had at school! I travelled to her city a week later. Once there, she asked me to accompany her to the prison to give a two-hour workshop, for two days, for the prisoners deprived of their freedom. I was afraid, enough to ask her for a few days before giving her an answer. That night in my room, I knelt down and prayed to God for a long time.

The next day my answer was clear:

If I face fear itself, there will be no other fear that will stop me!

Instead of fear, let us always opt for mercy and love.

WOMEN LIVING FEARLESSLY

SUNRISE

Crossing the walls of the prison, to enter an unknown universe, was an experience that began with fear. Knowing I was not alone, because Sister Gloria was with me, gave me security.

The day was rainy and cold, the guards guarding the maximum-security facility, serious, the long corridors seemed endless, the bars thick and imposing. Forty men, prisoners prepared for the meeting, sitting in a circle around us inside the room, was a challenging image. I prayed to God to give me wisdom. I took a deep breath and greeted saying:

'Brothers, you suffer and cry in this place deprived of your freedom, I suffer being free outside of here. I am free in body, but my soul is still in unknown prisons. I am here to help you. Together we will design products that you can sell and have money to help your family. We will work with our hands to heal the soul and dry our tears together.'

At the end of the fall, I had a meeting with the prison leaders. The news was terrible; there was no budget for the materials they needed. I understood I had to act immediately. I went to schools asking them to provide me with office paper that they didn't need. I visited a television channel and appealed to citizens, so the materials they did not want, such as paper, cardboard and other recyclable products, were taken to the prison. *Divine miracle!* The next day the trucks began to arrive with materials such as paper, cardboard, colours or pencils. Although this was not enough. I decided to consult the prisoners and ask them what they had. Their response was not very encouraging:

We only have chicken bones, beef bones and bull horns.

We will make designs with them! Don't be sad! ... Do you have wood?

Only splinters and small pieces that measure no more than 3cm, and sawdust.

And fabrics or threads?

No. Just leftover threads, wool and some scraps of fabric.

Alright. You have to select and separate the wood by size, put the sawdust in bags, dry the chicken bones, cow bones and bull horns in the sun. I will bring some other products.

I came back in a week. We started making charms, bracelets, rings and earrings with bull bones and chunks. The next day, unused clothing arrived at the prison, and we began to work removing the buttons, zippers and collars from the shirts. We began to make fabric pillows and blankets, proposing a project to design quilts and their covers. Postcards, cards, angels and spheres for Christmas trees were created with recycled cardboard and paper.

I went to visit the sheriff in charge of the prison with the proposal to design a small garden, so the inmates could grow healing plants for the most common ailments, such as stomach pain, headaches or high blood pressure. I presented the biogarden project in the form of platforms, like in the time of the Incas, with irrigation canals so that water is not lost and is used to the last plant. Christmas was approaching, time was passing quickly when Sister Gloria worriedly asked:

'Sofia, who will sell these products? We have to set up a small fair and sell them, for them.'

I accepted and we started selling the first products. In a week, we had everything sold. I took a deep breath and remembered the verses from the book of Psalms:

'Inexhaustible love and truth met
Justice and peace kissed.
The truth springs from the earth,
And justice smiles from the heavens.'

The day I said goodbye to Gloria, because I was returning home, I hugged her with deep love, affirming that I had already found my path and that this was to serve others. I still remember our eyes wet with tears, the first Christmas carols echoing in the distance, the windows decorated with coloured lights and the rain that was beginning to splash. Before getting on the bus to Lima, I walked smiling through the streets for a while, with my heart full of love and gratitude towards God.

Only by helping others do we get away from our own problems and see the positive impact we can have on the lives of others.

UNIQUE PERSONAL JOURNEY

My heart was disassembling the prisons I had in my soul. They faded as the weeks went by, and I began to live a life celebrating small victories, finding joy in the little things and trusting in God's will.

I changed houses. I went to live in an apartment with a beautiful tree nearby, whose leaves shone in the reflection of the sun. Potted gerberas and geraniums intertwine. I started a new life, my hands got lost between designs and sculptures; between the violin and my dreams. I won many awards because I kept my heart and mind focused on others, serving them and transforming their lives. My hands were butterflies, landing on many faces to heal wounds. My chest was a refuge for many children.

Practicing love brings us closer to the heart of God. My feet do not stop walking, forging the dream of helping invisible artists, artists without limbs, in wheelchairs, deaf and blind, because I think of them with the dignity of their courage, and I walk with perseverance. Serving others helps to regain happiness and transform life.

Living a full and happy life strengthens our relationship with God. Pain is not a punishment but a gift. Gratitude and love cannot be missing in a life where mercy is a source of peace.

I am an entrepreneur, designer, lawyer and inventor in Lima, Peru. I serve as the general manager and head of the department of the international magazine *The Designer* in Peru, and I bring my culture to the world through *The Designer*. My vision, hard work and determination led me to extend the magazine to the brother country of Colombia in Cali and Cartago, weaving cultures, customs and art. *The Desginer* is an art and culture magazine based in Stockholm, Sweden.

I earned second place worldwide with the 'Magic Sphere' in 2015, being a finalist in design with 'Tray Girax' in 2016, getting the winning banner in my country with 'No More Lives Lost' in 2017, creating a company called 'Markku's Design Company' in 2018, carrying out product design projects and workshops in prisons in 2019, participating in the international Kiwie contest, organised in Korea in 2020, inventing 'A personal protection garment with joining elements for beauty centres', silver medal in Kiwie in 2021. Most importantly, I was invited to the Tigullio Design District TDD in 2022, the most glamorous event in Liguria, Italy, to present the most experienced designers, and was chosen as a panel member of the Kultura Project Italy in 2023.

Recently, I became a member of the Women Leaders of the Americas, the Afro-Andean Board of Trustees for Culture and Development in Peru, and Remart, an international network of women artists in Medellin, Colombia. She just joined the Top Level Global Relations Platform as Peru's ambassador.

Most recently, I won the 2024 Women Changing the World Award and was recognised as a cultural manager in the area of communications by the Andean Parliament.

MY STORY 'BUNYANDYI GILANG'

Tara Croker

Another day, another meeting. Discussing metrics, targets, the usual, but this time my boss concluded the meeting with a passing comment 'we're not saving lives'. After more than ten years in the corporate space as a marketing professional in some of Australia's leading organisations, and now working at one of the biggest and well-known global companies, my boss' words were meant to remind the team to value our wellbeing. But they inspired me into thinking how I wanted to do something more meaningful, something with purpose. Something that could not only inspire me but others too. It may sound a little corny, but I did want to make a difference; I wanted to create something that would contribute to a more connected world.

I'd had an idea bubbling away, for a number of years, about starting my own business and creating something unique. But having the courage to do something about it would mean *living fearlessly*, right? It would take courage to leave a successful career, stability and certainty, but I also felt that as much as I loved my job, I couldn't see myself working for someone else for another thirty years.

As a proud *Wiradjuri yinaa*, it goes without saying that I've always had a strong connection to the land. My mum (also my business partner) and I are both big plant lovers and foodies. We've always grown our own food, and I continue to grow a variety of plants, including native Australian plants. I've always loved playing around in the kitchen using traditional plants to flavour drinks, like the pure lemon myrtle tea I drink most days. For a couple of years, we'd been experimenting with all sorts of things, even going down to our local brewery to use their facilities to brew beers, ciders and ginger beer using native plants.

I did some research and shockingly discovered that Indigenous representation in the native food supply chain is less than 2%. Non-Indigenous businesses were using native plant knowledge in their products, without returning any of the economic benefits to where this knowledge comes from. The fire within was lit – I wanted to turn the tables and authentically share these flavours with a sustainable and community-driven approach.

And it's grown from there.

FROM SEED TO RECIPE 'MARRAMARRA GUMBALANG GAMBIRRA'

I wanted to go beyond just 'Australian-made' and delve into the genuine connection with Indigenous culture and the true taste of native ingredients; to give people real exposure to what plants taste like in this country. But to do it authentically and sustainably, coming from the community and telling the stories behind those plants.

We had a lot to do to create the product, having delicious recipes didn't mean we had something to sell – and it wasn't an easy ride. Armed with my years of marketing experience, it was now time to deep dive into the manufacturing and operations side of business.

During the ideation phase, there was a large amount of time spent finding a production partner that could provide the expertise we were looking for. Beverage manufacturers are few and far between, especially when you're starting out and producing smaller quantities. Our product development started just before the pandemic which complicated the process and forced us to rely solely on remote collaboration rather than getting into the lab. When testing the recipe flavour levels, they had to send us samples by post which extended the process. Navigating the male-dominated manufacturing industry as a female entrepreneur also presented challenges. Ultimately, the company we engaged for the original trial product just couldn't provide the expertise we were looking for.

We made plans to meet directly with them, and soon realised they weren't up to the task. It turned out to be quite a challenge, with some legal involvement, but it wasn't long before the manufacturer actually ended up going out of business. Not just from our challenge, but because they had sadly created similar situations with several other startups.

So, there we were, two years down and basically starting from scratch. My dream becoming a reality seemed increasingly out of reach.

It's in times like these that you need the tenacity to knuckle-down, solve the problem and go again. You must truly believe in and know your big vision and mission, to keep the fire burning. We had bootstrapped the business and used all our own funds to this point, so I guess it could have been an easy time to give up, but the thought never crossed my mind. We still had amazing recipes, and we would take them elsewhere. The final products became everything we dreamed they would be.

I now had two delicious flavours, completely natural and sugar-free, honouring the true flavours my ancestors have enjoyed for generations. Working with Indigenous wild harvesters and local farmers, I knew we had a sustainable and environmentally conscious plant supply for our drinks. Working alongside Indigenous artists and designers, we were able to tell our authentic story and respectfully represent the plants using the bottles as our canvas.

All that was left was to sell the product!

THE NEXT STEP 'GULAYGAN'

Launching the website in early 2023, we had only been in business a few months when we successfully applied to appear on *Shark Tank*, which went on to air later that year.

As I grabbed Mum's hand, walking along the corridor heading into the stress-inducing Shark Tank, I was desperately trying to push down what felt like a million butterflies in my stomach. We kept our smiles wide as we entered the room. We knew we had one chance at getting the funding we needed to produce our drink product to scale. We'd funded our startup ourselves to this point, and we were so proud of what we'd created, but landing investment would help take us to the next phase. Facing the Sharks, I somehow found the courage to speak, though I could feel my heart rate skyrocket and the slight quiver of nervousness in my voice. I was able to relax as the opening conversation seemed to be going well. We did have an amazing product, after all – visually beautiful and delicious to taste – the Sharks really enjoyed the flavours too. I felt positive energy from the Sharks and my confidence returned as they questioned us one after the other for almost two hours. Then I was hit with the question – 'What marketing have you done so far?' I faltered. I mean, I was still working full-time as a marketing professional at one of the biggest companies in the world. I knew we hadn't undertaken paid marketing activities because we had only soft launched weeks before filming. We were still in the early days being as savvy and scrappy as possible. For instance, seeking no-cost PR from a national television program … but I couldn't say that to the people I was trying to get investment from on that very program, so I mentioned our website and organic social activity, but it felt like lip-service. One by one the Sharks started to fall, but somehow, all our fears were silenced, as we managed to work out a deal with exactly the right people. It was just meant to be.

The Sharks believed in us, our products and our brand, and we couldn't have been happier. We now had the foundations and expert coaching needed to build the business of our dreams, sharing the unique tastes of Australia in every sip, and not just nationally, but eventually internationally too.

As you can imagine, being featured on national television creates a certain amount of interest. In a flourish, there were plenty of media opportunities and an incredible amplification of the brand and our mission, leading to customers all over the country and plenty of international requests. This highlighted our need to grow our distribution channels and improve our fulfilment costs. As we grow, we're working closely with our suppliers to collectively build Indigenous businesses and remain authentic with our mission and values.

REFLECTIONS 'WINHANGADURINYA'

Protecting our native plants from commercial exploitation and ensuring Indigenous voices remain at the forefront of the native food industry is a complex challenge that must be addressed systemically. While the broader market has embraced native ingredients, it's crucial to maintain cultural integrity and ownership. The journey to establish Yaala Sparkling gave me first-hand experience in the challenges faced by Indigenous entrepreneurs. I guess there is an element of fear around these factors, in that it's greater than me, but I just need to live in the *yaala* (present moment). At the heart of Yaala is the deep craving to reconnect people with our local environment including our native plants and the age-old, yet timeless, stories and knowledge of our land. We do this in the hope, if only in a small way, to be a catalyst for transforming connection and meaning – with each other, with nature and within ourselves.

The overwhelming support from our community and customers has been a driving force. Sharing our passion for native flavours and contributing to Indigenous empowerment has created a powerful sense of purpose. The entrepreneurial journey is a steep learning curve. Transitioning from a corporate role to building a business from the ground up demands versatility and resilience. Every challenge, from securing funding to managing inventory, becomes a lesson in adaptability and I approach every lesson with a growth mindset. Surrounding myself with a supportive network of fellow founders and mentors has been invaluable in navigating this path. It has been inspiring to connect with other people who share the same vision of building a better future for everyone.

So, if you've got an idea, a dream of a higher purpose, or you're an entrepreneur just starting out, remember to be resilient, tenacious and patient. There's no doubt there will be setbacks along the way, but don't give up on your vision and passion, and surround yourself with others who believe it too.

Respect the earth, because it is a sacred thing.

Yindyamarra bangalbuwurayi, yanhagi nganhagu minyambul yiri yirimbang.

TARA CROKER
Artist: Tiaan Shutt, Worimi

Tara Croker, a proud First Nations Wiradjuri woman, is a trailblazing entrepreneur who seamlessly merges her Indigenous heritage with the dynamic world of business.

Her impressive career trajectory includes coveted roles in high-profile global corporations such as Google, YouTube and News Corp, where she honed her business acumen and marketing expertise.

Driven by a deep-rooted passion for the land and community, Tara founded Yaala Sparkling, an innovative beverage company that celebrates the rich flavours of native Australian plants. She not only promotes sustainable and healthy practices, but also strives to increase First Nations participation within the native food industry. This manifests in her commitment to sourcing ingredients from local wild harvesters and suppliers, then collaborating with Indigenous artists to tell the authentic story of the plants. With each sip of Yaala Sparkling, consumers embark on a journey of cultural discovery, savouring the authentic flavours that have sustained Indigenous communities for generations. Tara's vision for Yaala Sparkling is twofold: to increase First Nations representation in the native food industry and to authentically connect people to native Australian plants.

Tara's entrepreneurial journey has been marked by significant milestones, including a successful pitch on Shark Tank and numerous awards recognising her business acumen. Beyond her professional accomplishments, she is a dedicated advocate for reconciliation efforts, mentoring new leaders and sitting on boards and advisory committees. Tara's story is a testament to the power of combining cultural heritage with business innovation offering a unique perspective on leadership, entrepreneurship and meaningful impact.

TARA CROKER

Awards:
- Naturally Good Awards, Best New Brand | 2024 Finalist
- Small Business Champion Awards, Indigenous Business of the Year | 2024 Winner
- Minderoo DreamVenture Showcase | 2024 Winner
- Young Hero Awards | 2024 Finalist
- Women Leading Tech Awards | 2024 Finalist
- Online Retail Industry Awards | 2024 Finalist
- Named on B&T Women's Power List 2024
- First Nations Bushfood Alliance Awards, Excellence in Marketing & Cultural Storytelling | 2024 Winner
- She-Com Awards, First Nations Business of the Year | 2024 Winner
- She-Com Awards, Beverage Product of the Year | 2024 Finalist
- First Nations Gold Awards, Best New Brand | 2024 Winner
- University of Queensland Entrepreneurship & Innovation Awards, Beverage Start-up of the Year | 2024 Finalist
- Women's Agenda Leadership Awards | 2023 Finalist

Qualifications:
- Bachelor of Business Administration, Australian Catholic University, Australia
- Bachelor of Global Studies, University of Bradford, United Kingdom
- Beyond Strategic Planning, Harvard University, America

ROARING INTO AUTHENTICITY

Tiffany James

There is a universal thirst to be a better version of ourselves. Could it be on the account that, as we sit before expansive auditorium screens or spellbound by the fine dark ink that structures experiences one could just dream of in the books we read, we realise that we were created for a purpose bigger than ourselves? There are numerous lessons to be learned from the superheroes we grew up watching on the big screen to the historical figures we've read about. Not to mention, the unpredictable journey of the ordinary, run-of-the-mill person, who ends up inspiring us that the possibility of fulfilling our purpose is not a distant dream. There is a familiar axiom, that there is a *you* that you have never met. It is said that the issues that provoke us the most are often the ones we are meant to address. Under immense pressure, the hero within us emerges.

From an early age, I was deeply troubled by seeing anyone overlooked or mistreated for not measuring up or fitting into societal norms. I used to think I was overly sensitive, but I came to realise it was because I could deeply relate to the pain of being rejected and feeling invisible. Not invisible in the sense of not being physically seen but invisible in the sense that my thoughts, emotions and personality were often overlooked, overshadowed by the facade I felt compelled to present in a world that valued conformity over authenticity.

I spent years suppressing a vital part of myself – a powerful force within that I feared and didn't fully understand. It was like a lion, caged deep inside me, occasionally stirring but never truly free. This force longed to roar, to reveal its true strength and vulnerability, yet it remained trapped, pacing with frustration. It wasn't until my mid-to-late-forties that I finally let that lion roar, unleashing the brave girl inside me.

TIFFANY JAMES

When we think of a lion, we imagine its courage, strength and fearlessness. But true freedom requires more than just courage; it demands a rebellion against the norm. We all have this courageous spirit within us, often lying dormant, waiting for the right moment to break free.

Growing up, I was constantly bombarded with messages within and outside of my home that made me doubt my place in the world. I struggled with the pain of rejection. I longed to belong, to be accepted by the people and community I was born into, but didn't choose. This longing for acceptance consumed me because one doesn't truly crave it until we feel its absence, and that absence created a void in my life. I believe, despite our differences, each of us eventually arrives at a place where external forces start to chip away at our inner sense of self. This leads to a gnawing discontent, a persistent feeling of not measuring up, of being somehow less than enough. We learn to live with this feeling as if it were a permanent companion. It can manifest as a restless conscience, a nagging sense of inadequacy or intrusive thoughts that pop into our heads uninvited. It's profoundly sad to live within a question mark of one's own existence, never fully present or at ease in the rooms you walk into.

Being an African American woman born in the early seventies, I rarely saw anyone who looked like me in the media. Television was a landscape populated by faces and stories that did not reflect my own reality. In school, the heroes in the books we read were overwhelmingly white, presenting yet another layer of exclusion that told me, implicitly, that I was destined for mediocrity. I was being conditioned to believe that no matter how hard I worked, my accomplishments and success were constrained by my experience accompanied by what white-America would allow. It was as though there was an invisible boundary that I dared not cross – a boundary that dictated my worth and potential. But what happens when a lion is conditioned to believe it was created only to be caged? What happens when everything that defines its true nature, its authority, its freedom and its inherent power is suppressed? Eventually, a lion, after being caged for so long, can no longer be contained. It shows its true nature, rooted in freedom, strength and dominance. The confinement clashes with its inherent desire to live as it was meant to, creating an unstoppable urge to break free. Just as the lion's spirit refuses to be tamed indefinitely, human potential, when suppressed, eventually demands liberation, pushing us to overcome barriers and reclaim our true selves. The challenge is that each time the lion tries to break free in attempts to step beyond the confines of its captivity, a captor stands ready to rein it in, to imprison it once more.

In the metaphor of the lion, I see a reflection of my own journey. Each time I dared to express my true self, an invisible force pulled me back, whispering that my dreams were too grand and my aspirations too ambitious for someone like me; a young Black girl with thick hair, wearing hand-me-downs and off-brand clothes from the South Side of Chicago, born to hardworking, barely middle-class parents. This wasn't just a momentary feeling – it was a persistent, unrelenting battle within, a constant struggle between the person I was told to be and the person I knew I was meant to become.

As I navigated through the maze of life, I began to realise that the cage I found myself in wasn't solely crafted by external forces. It wasn't just societal expectations, rejection or the deep-seated wound of shame from being molested in the supposed safety of my own home by a cousin I adored. It wasn't just the emotional and mental abuse I endured in my early twenties when I fell in love with a man I loved more than myself. It wasn't even the countless, unseen termites gnawing away at whatever self-worth I had left. No, this cage was also of my own making, forged by years of internalised doubt and ingrained beliefs about what I could and couldn't achieve, accompanied by the pride and shame that refused to allow me to admit my truth and seek healing. This was a psychological prison, constructed from the bricks of every 'you're not good enough' I had ever heard or felt. Each brick carried a message that reinforced the notion that I needed to fit into a mould not designed for me – a mould that was too confining, too small for the person I truly was inside.

It demanded a confrontation with every deeply held belief that had told me to play small, to quiet my voice, to accept less than what I deserved. As this courage awakened, I began to question the validity of those invisible chains that held me back. Were they truly real? Or were they simply illusions created by my mind, fed by years of societal programming, rejection and personal insecurity? I started to dissect these chains, examining each link to understand its origin and its hold over me. With each revelation, the chains began to loosen, and I felt the weight of my self-imposed limitations lift. It was a transformative process, one that required honesty and introspection, demanding I confront the deepest fears, doubts and pain that I had harboured for so long.

As I broke free from societal expectations and the toxic narratives I had internalised, I began to truly own my story and embrace my gifts. I didn't embark on this journey of healing and self-discovery alone. My faith in God and the trusted individuals He placed in my life (those with whom I could be vulnerable and unashamed) empowered me. With them, I didn't have to sugarcoat my story or hide behind a facade.

The journey of inner healing is powerful and enduring. Through introspection, I identified the chains that held me captive: comparison, competition and criticism. I realised these forces not only tethered me but also countless others to societal expectations, dimming our light and preventing us from embracing our true selves.

Societal standards, often vague yet persistently reinforced by media, popularity and messaging, become the unspoken benchmarks for success. When the majority endorses something, it quickly sets the standard, creating immense pressure. This pressure fuels an internal struggle, compelling us to compare ourselves to others and becomes the breeding ground for self-doubt.

Competition has become an unhealthy obsession to prove that our unique gifts are superior to others', rather than using it to sharpen and inspire one another while celebrating our unique contributions to the world. When our focus shifts from being our best to being better than someone else, we become puppets with society pulling the strings, judging our worth. Imagine standing before a jury of strangers every week, sentenced and imprisoned by their constantly changing opinions of what it means to be the prettiest, smartest, fastest, strongest or most skilled, etc. This life sentence of comparison prevents us from living authentically or even truly living at all.

For years, I struggled to be myself because I was trapped in comparison. In every room I entered, my internal sight judged how others viewed me. Bombarded by the same question: *Do I measure up to their expectations of me?* I needed the masses to validate my self-perception before I could truly believe in it myself. This constant need for validation kept me from truly enjoying the present or embracing the amazing opportunities in my life. When we compare ourselves, we edit the original version of who we are, trying to fit into a mould never meant for us. We become dissatisfied with our lives. While aspirations are healthy, when driven by someone else's success, we end up in a one-sided competition with a person unaware of our battle. Worse, we unknowingly fight against ourselves. This cycle leads to self-criticism and judgement of others. We wake up with discontentment, lacking joy in our journey. Our paths become dictated by others' opinions and approval, measuring our success against a standard set by strangers. This diminishes our self-worth and can lead us to forfeit our true destinies.

The pressure to conform often drives us into emotional, financial, and mental debt. Like me, we may form superficial relationships with people who don't truly know or appreciate us. In seeking external validation, we lose sight of who we are and what truly matters. But here's the truth: we are not meant to live in the shadow of others. Our journeys are uniquely ours. By breaking free from comparison, competition and criticism, we can live authentically and joyfully, but more importantly purposefully.

This is not an easy task when you are coming against the masses. It requires courage to confront uncomfortable truths, yet this courage sparks true transformation. By embracing and sharing our narratives, we inspire others to do the same. This became my mission: not just to liberate myself, but to help others break free from self and societal constraints. It wasn't enough for me to be liberated, like Harriet Tubman, I felt compelled to risk everything to help others break free from their own self-imposed and societal chains. I began by living my truth, sharing my story and embracing myself fully. I practiced being present, not editing myself to fit in and daring to rebel against the norm despite the risk of being overlooked or misunderstood.

I created safe spaces for honest, vulnerable conversations and became an encouragement coach, helping women discover their unique voices and walk confidently in their destinies. I wanted every woman who crossed my path to feel seen, heard and valued. By having uncomfortable conversations and challenging women to find joy beyond external validation, I aimed to teach the power of simply being. I learned that embracing our greatness allows us to celebrate others more deeply.

To support this mission, I launched my one-day retreat called You Belong in the Room. The retreat was designed to empower women to know they belong in the spaces they are invited into, and if their value isn't recognised, they might just be in the wrong room. Don't change yourself, change the rooms that don't recognise your greatness.

Simultaneously, I introduced my You Belong in the Room encouragement boxes, which feature my own work alongside the creations of other talented women. These boxes spotlight women who, despite not having physical stores, large followings or big marketing budgets, have incredible gifts to offer. By showcasing their products, I celebrate their brilliance in the rooms I'm blessed to be in. This endeavour has brought me immense joy.

WOMEN LIVING FEARLESSLY

If I had more time, I'd share the incredible testimonies I've received over the years. Though I've had the privilege of being an author, encouragement coach and performing spoken word, motivational speaking and more, across states and other countries, nothing compares to the joy of loving who God created me to be. It took over forty years to uncover this profound truth, but once I did, I realised that our doing flows from our being, defying all limitations.

As I reflect on this journey, I am overwhelmed with gratitude. This journey has been a profound gift, one I hope to continue to share with the world, so that others will find the courage to live their truth as well, understanding that our stories, with all their complexities and imperfections, shape us and open doors to endless possibilities.

Embracing our true selves means harnessing the courage of a lion, breaking free from the chains of comparison, competition and criticism. It allows us to live freely and joyfully, celebrating our unique paths without the need for external validation. Our collective journey is just beginning and I am excited to see where it takes us.

Together, let us walk with the boldness of a lion, courageously embracing our true selves and rejecting imposed standards. By celebrating our individuality and that of others, we unlock new possibilities and inspire others to do the same – this is the epitome of roaring into authenticity.

Meet Tiffany James, the dynamic founder of Encouraging Touch Enterprises. A seasoned motivational speaker, writer, coach, emcee, spoken word artist and storyteller, Tiffany is dedicated to inspiring individuals to embrace their authentic selves and confidently navigate life's diverse spaces. She is unwavering in her commitment to ensuring that everyone she meets feels genuinely, seen, heard and valued. She encourages others to recognise their potential, walk in their purpose and celebrate their greatness while uplifting those around them.

Family holds a special place in Tiffany's heart, as she is happily married and a proud mother of three beautiful now adult daughters. Tiffany's journey took a transformative turn in 2007 when her corporate career ended abruptly. Undeterred, she followed her true passion for using her voice and writing to inspire change. Her personal experiences with overcoming uncertainties and disappointments give her a deep understanding of the challenges faced by those pursuing their dreams. With unwavering faith in God, self-determination and a resilient support system, Tiffany emerged stronger and now serves as a guiding light for others. Fuelled by unwavering faith and determination, she returned to school, earning a BA in English with a minor in creative writing just shy of her forty-ninth birthday, proving that it's never too late to follow your dreams.

During the same period of time, in line with her mission, Tiffany has introduced the 'You Belong in the Room' encouragement one-day retreats and boxes. These retreats create a safe space for women to embrace their true authentic selves, while the unique boxes feature her book, *Living in the Land of I Am – Your Life Story Reveals your Purpose*,

TIFFANY JAMES

along with personalised poetry postcards. Most importantly, these boxes spotlight other female entrepreneurs, allowing talented women without brick-and-mortar stores to be showcased and celebrated. Through these boxes, Tiffany feels she is taking these women into the rooms she has been invited into, supporting their businesses and highlighting their talents.

Through workshops, storytelling, encouragement coaching, speaking engagements and her inspiring book, Tiffany consistently imparts her message of embracing who you are created to be. A dynamic speaker who commands the stage, she believes that success isn't solely measured by financial figures but by the courage to remain true to oneself while pursuing purpose. Her mentoring philosophy echoes, 'Greatness is about serving others with the gift that God has given you.' Tiffany James invites you to embrace your journey and discover the power of your purpose.

Recognised for her dedication and impact, Tiffany is the winner of the 2024 International Women Changing the World in Personal Service award.

THE GIFT OF SILENCE

Veronica (Vee) Haslam

O*kay, draw your lifeline,* was the instruction ... I can do that! How hard can it be?

I mean, my life had been fairly ordinary, right? Pretty straightforward. And ... That was where it began.

My chaotic, emotional, transformative journey began at twenty-seven, when I was blessed with the opportunity to pursue a postgraduate course. This two-year program focused on innovation, self-awareness, group dynamics ... and change.

One of my mentors, at the time, had completed the course. He was the best people manager I'd ever met! I was inspired by him. He'd shared that the course was about self-awareness, and I was so ready for that!

Well, at least that's what I thought.

Let's rewind a few days, before it began.

It was 2002, and I was driving on a beautiful coastal road. It literally felt like the sun was shining and the birds were singing. We were to spend a whole week in residence, beside the beach, learning more about ourselves! I couldn't wait to see what amazing insights I was to discover.

When we settled into our learning space, we sat on chairs in a big circle without desks. It was different from the conventional classroom or lecture theatre. As we began to share discussions, it became clear there were to be no set readings, exams or assignments for the year. This was not what I had expected at all! Having been to school and university, I had my own clear idea of what being a 'student' meant, but this was completely unfamiliar!

While this might seem like a dream course for some, for me, being in the unfamiliar triggered inner confusion.

VERONICA (VEE) HASLAM

We would sit together in silence at the beginning of the day; an open space for any emerging thoughts or reflections. Sometimes nothing was said, or occasionally, a reflection on a dream or something previously discussed would be shared. All very unpredictable in nature ... and all very foreign to me.

All I could think was, *I have no idea what I'm meant to say.*

All I could feel was my frustration at myself ... *Why couldn't I say anything?*

As I sat in that circle, my inner critic started screaming inside my head, while on the outside, I was mostly silent. And soon, it didn't matter if we were sitting in the quiet reflective part of the day or if we were in a topical discussion, sitting in that circle made me instantly feel, in both my body and my mind, that I was the only one who didn't understand what was happening and had nothing valuable to contribute.

And it was here, deep in the fear of what the silence held, that I began to unwrap the gift.

I had NO idea of what was expected of me.

... or what I needed to DO to be a good student.

What did this mean?

Well, that brings me to drawing my lifeline.

My life had been good. I was an ABC (Australian-born Chinese). I had two loving parents, two younger sisters and a dog. We were a middle-class family, and my parents had worked hard to provide us with educational and life opportunities. I played the piano. I was married and was a project director. My lifeline was going to be very straightforward.

As we sat in that circle over the next few days, there was no set order for presenting our lifelines. Each student stood up whenever they felt ready, picking up their paper, and so it continued for the twenty or so of us.

Our program director shared a very personal story as the first lifeline shared. That set the tone for what was to come; lifeline stories which felt, to me, to be so much more significant than mine. Some people had lived through some heavy stuff. And I felt that mine was NOT eventful, at all.

Finally, I picked up my paper and stood in front of the group, being the last to present. My voice was shaking, and I can't even recall what I said. After I finished, I went to the beach to sit alone and broke down, in uncontrollable tears.

What was going on?

Why was I so upset?

The program director asked what was going on for me and all I could muster up, between the hyperventilating breaths was, *'I don't know.'*

For the next two years, sitting in that circle revealed my deepest vulnerabilities. I often sat there without being able to say anything, trapped in the chaotic emotions that my suffocating silence held.

It was later I learned that the ingenious course design was to dismantle your known structures so you were left without familiar constructs to:

- Place your own sense of identity within.
- Understand how your perception of role affects your behaviours.
- Know who you are.

Getting to know myself meant peeling away the external influences that had shaped who I was without my realising it. It began with dismantling who I thought I should be as a 'student'. If I didn't know what was expected, how could I meet the expectations?

And when I didn't know how to meet expectations, I went silent.

I lost my voice.

I became critical of myself.

I felt I had nothing to offer.

Gift one: When I didn't know what was expected of me, I didn't know who to be.

This sparked my quest to explore what the silence held for me. And a bit like a pass-the-parcel, the more I've unwrapped, the more unexpected gifts I've found.

VERONICA (VEE) HASLAM

A few years before my postgraduate course experience, I remember walking down the aisle to get married. My husband-to-be was a good person. We had been together for a few years, he had bought a house, I had finished my degree and was working in my second professional job. Marriage seemed like the next logical step; so that's what we did. I remember arriving in a beautiful vintage wedding car with my grandparents, dad, sisters and me in front of the bluestone church. Though neither of us were religious, we thought marriage happened in a bluestone church.

As the wedding car parked, I saw my girlfriend's mum on the church steps. She was the only one I noticed, as most guests had gone inside. She was excitedly taking photos. As soon as I saw her, I started to cry and kept my feelings silent. She was the only parent of our friendship group who was divorced. At the time, I didn't know why a feeling of sadness came over me. As life would reveal, the tears in my silence held a deeper knowing, that I was doing something that I thought I *should* do; meeting expectations of the path that I thought I was meant to take, rather than listening to the whispers of my soul.

Gift two: My emotion in the silence reveals inner truths.

After having two kids and reaching the milestones I had expected, I found myself feeling numb in my marriage. I decided to divorce and went on my first retreat. As I arrived at the retreat residence, it looked smaller than I had imagined. Despite reading that it was 'exclusive', I had assumed there would be other attendees. The lovely couple who owned the retreat greeted me at the driveway and showed me to my accommodation. It quickly became clear that I was the only guest.

I flicked through the itinerary and saw there would be windows of time that were not allocated to any activity. What could I do? Where should I go? Should I visit the township? After all, I was a tourist.

There lay the third gift being revealed.

For the next six days, the retreat owners focused on nourishing, nurturing and healing me. Instead of touring, there were many moments of journalling and contemplation. I found solace in being alone in the retreat space, embracing the silence. It gave me room to reconnect with parts of myself I had deeply buried. Recurring dreams from when I was around ten years old resurfaced, and I shed tears as I allowed myself to heal. Old, suppressed emotions flowed out of me in ways I hadn't known possible. Through meditation, narrative therapy and sound healing, I connected to a deeper sense of awareness that I had never experienced before.

Gift three: The freedom to reflect in silence and being compassionately witnessed by another allowed me to acknowledge, honour and release old blockages.

A flashback to a significant childhood memory then resurfaced, while I was saving some very old family videos to my computer. Mum had shared these, and they included beautiful moments of our extended family and trips overseas. Among the footage, was my birthday party from when I was around six years old. Watching it, I was reminded of how the party shifted from being so much fun, dancing around the house, to a moment when I felt overwhelmed with shame.

It came back to me as the earliest moment I remember going silent. It was at the end of the birthday party when I had soiled my pants. I walked around without telling anyone, not even my mum. Unsure of what to do, I eventually tried to clean it up in the toilet. The memory, both in my mind and body, was marked by a deep sense of shame.

Gift four: Our childhood experiences are stored in our emotional and energetic being. When we're ready, clues to releasing what no longer serves us will emerge.

As I embarked on starting my own business in 2019, I found myself drawn to a mindfulness-based stillness meditation teacher training course. It wasn't something I had planned, but it felt like the right next step. As I immersed myself in the program, I fluctuated between grappling with the concepts and practicing the teachings. Reading the guided meditation scripts during role-play exercises felt more like reciting pages from a book in front of a classroom than guiding a meditative practice. In the hours of silent meditation, I felt into the gap between merely reading about the concepts and truly understanding them. The silence was helping me expand my practice of awareness and embodiment.

Gift five: The difference between concept and embodiment is the practice of experiential learning.

As I continued to explore the depths of silence, I found myself on a six-day silent retreat. Shortly after arriving, I quickly grew comfortable with the silence. The retreat's rules allowed me to exist in my own world, while being around others. It was a fascinating experience eating meals in silence, next to and across from strangers. The lack of eye contact and the absence of small gestures like a smile or a thank you when the door was held open, or the food was served, stood out to me. These moments highlighted my own need for social connection and acceptance.

As I felt into this more in the hours of silent meditation, I could see the parts of myself that were looking for acknowledgement from the other. To be reassured that I had been seen. When I knew that it wasn't about me and that I was okay just being in the space as it was, I realised I didn't need others to 'see' or 'acknowledge' me.

Gift six: When we look to the external for something we feel lacking in, we are really looking for it within ourselves.

Over the past five years, bringing my heartful leadership work to life has held many moments of self-doubt. I have sometimes wondered if I know enough to share. I have wondered if what I'm passionate about is of any interest to the corporate world. After all, talking about *feeling into our humanness and leading in a heartful* way is not yet a common agenda item.

Working on my own, the silence has been profound. Often, I have felt like I am standing on the side of the Grand Canyon and screaming out what I feel matters, and all I have heard are echoes. Producing video content, newsletters, posts, service products, spending tons of money and time on learning how to do something and then giving it a go, and it not working as I had intended. Many times, I believed an experiment would be 'the one' that succeeded, only to discover the next step demanded another deep breath and the courage to move forward.

In the silence of not receiving immediate validation from a boss or others, I've discovered the need to find my inner resilience and stay committed to my greater purpose. I've realised that what I'm doing is not about me; it's about something bigger. It's a privilege to be part of bringing that to life. Through the silence I have felt creativity and flow, knowing they are not from me, but through me. That my abundance is in the freedom to be; to allow my mission to come through me for our collective abundance for all.

Gift seven: Without external validation, I discovered a deep knowing that my purpose is to let what is working through me flow.

This brings me to the present. Given my challenges in intimate relationships, I've questioned whether I can truly connect with a man from a place of unconditional love. I've been with my partner, Gerry, for nearly six years, but the past couple of years have felt disconnected. We've faced significant health issues, which have affected how we individually and collectively show up in our relationship. While my work with others often explores recurring limiting patterns, I've felt stuck in my own blind spots within this intimate space. I reached a point where I needed to understand whether Gerry and I had what it takes to continue growing together. It felt important not only for our relationship but also for my work mission.

So, we went on a couples retreat and spent seven days exploring loving presence and awareness together. A significant activity was eye gazing. We stood opposite each other and looked into each other's eyes for extended periods of time. Sometimes emotions would well up without a clear reason, and other times, we struggled to feel a connection. The key insight was that before we could deeply connect with each other, we needed to be connected to ourselves, what bestselling author and leading authority on human sexuality, Diana Richardson, calls 'our home'.

As we disconnected from our devices and work, and connected with each other through presence and awareness, I found the answer to my question. I felt it in the silence of looking into my partner's eyes. Being with him, with or without my defences, was okay. I didn't need to be anything, other than the deep truth of who I am, to be unconditionally loving. It was within me all along.

The silence we shared together in loving presence and awareness is what I feel is the latest gift.

Gift eight: Silence holds the revelation of truth. The truth in who we are, which is love.

I am deeply grateful for where the journey through silence has taken me over the years. As I reflect on this writing experience, I see there are many other gifts of silence that have shaped my path. I remain endlessly fascinated by how it might continue to reveal unexpected gifts as I explore this beautiful human experience. Thank you for sharing this moment with me.

Vee is passionate about connecting to the heart of the matter during times of change for greater wellbeing and performance. Vee's approach to leadership coaching enables her clients to curiously expand beyond rational thought by activating the mind, heart and spirit – making new discoveries and moving outside limitations held in their norm.

Take Einstein, for example. He uncovered incredible scientific discoveries while playing the violin. Vee's coaching philosophy and experiential approach embodies this concept. Exploring our human experiences through mindful and heartful awareness, clients can consciously explore inner transformation, which is vital in inspiring, leading and collaborating with others.

Vee has coached many individuals and worked with over forty teams in small to large organisations leading executive projects, the people-side of change, service improvement and team culture initiatives.

She is the founder of Heartful Leadership, the creator of The Power of Expression in Change program and the owner of The Heartful Leadership Global Learning Platform where she distills over two decades of inner work, her work with teams and leaders. She is currently the deputy chair of The Australian Transformation and Turnaround Association, TransformersUnite.com

Vee loves the magical unfolding of every day and expanding her learning in every moment. Her mission is to be part of co-creating a corporate paradigm where we share our unique gifts for an abundant world for all.

www.heartfulleadership.com.au

THIS BOOK CHANGES LIVES

Proceeds from the sale of this book go to providing marginalised women in business with scholarships to enable them to receive support, mentoring and education through The Women's Business School.

Aligning with the United Nations SDG goals for gender equality, The Women's Business School scholarships are awarded to women in remote and rural areas, First Nations women, migrant women, survivors of domestic violence, women with disability and chronic illness and those facing financial hardship.

We believe that investing in women is the most powerful way to change the world, and these scholarships provide opportunities for deserving women to participate in an incubator program for early stage startups and businesses and an accelerator program for high-potential entrepreneurs ready to scale their companies and expand globally.

You can read more about the work of The Women's Business School Scholarship Program and how they're changing the world here:

thewomensbusinessschool.com/scholarship

ABOUT PEACE & KATY AND SPEAKING OPPORTUNITIES

Peace and Katy are the dynamic duo behind AusMumpreneur, Australia's number-one community for mums in business; The Women's Business School, providing dedicated education for aspiring and established female founders; Women Changing the World Press, amplifying the voices of thought leaders, female founders and women changing the world; and Women Changing the World Investments, providing opportunities for capital for female founders.

Peace Mitchell is a TEDx speaker, international keynote speaker, retreat facilitator and workshop presenter.

If you want your audience to be captivated by a heart-centred, warm and engaging thought leader and speaker then look no further.

With experience delivering keynote presentations on connection, business success, magic and productivity, there's nothing Peace loves more than engaging with your delegates to make your event a huge success.

If you've got an online or in-person event coming up and want to create a magical, warm and engaging atmosphere, please get in touch.

peace@womensbusinesscollective.com
+61 431 615 107

ABOUT THE WOMEN'S BUSINESS SCHOOL

The Women's Business School is a business school designed exclusively for women. Providing opportunities for innovative female founders to scale their startup, connect with fellow founders and gain advice and guidance from successful entrepreneurs and experts. Through the award-winning incubator and accelerator programs, founders receive world-class entrepreneurial education from a team of high-level experts and entrepreneurs as well as mentoring, advice and access to successful female entrepreneurs across a range of industries. If you're ready to take your business to the next level apply today!

thewomensbusinessschool.com

ABOUT AUSMUMPRENEUR

Australia's number-one community for mumpreneurs. The AusMumpreneur Awards are a national event recognising and celebrating Australia's best and brightest mums in business. Held annually, these awards recognise the incredible women who are balancing business and motherhood and creating innovative, high-quality and remarkable brands across a range of industries.

ausmumpreneur.com

ABOUT WOMEN CHANGING THE WORLD PRESS

Women Changing the World Press publishes thought leaders, female founders and women who are committed to making the world a better place through their words and actions. We believe that investing in women is the most powerful way to change the world and we are passionate about amplifying women's voices, stories and ideas and providing more opportunities for women to share their message with the world. If you have a story that the world needs to hear get in touch today.

wcwpress.com

ABOUT WOMEN CHANGING THE WORLD AWARDS

The Women Changing the World Awards recognises, acknowledges and celebrates the trailblazers, changemakers and visionary action-takers. Providing a platform to amplify the achievements, accomplishments and work that women around the world are doing to make a difference in big and small ways. We believe that by elevating women, their ideas and their impact we can create a ripple effect that not only celebrates these women and the incredible work that they do but also inspires others to take action and make the world a better place in their own way too.

wcwawards.com

www.ingramcontent.com/pod-product-compliance
Lightning Source LLC
Chambersburg PA
CBHW060548080526
44585CB00013B/479